From Szatmar to the New World:
Max Wohlberg
American Cantor

From Szatmar to the New World:
Max Wohlberg
American Cantor

Charles Davidson

THE JEWISH THEOLOGICAL SEMINARY OF AMERICA
NEW YORK 2001

Acknowledgments

To Penny Aronson for her generous permission to include materials from her compilation of a Wohlberg bibliography for her master's degree from Gratz College; to the Cantors Assembly of America for permission to reprint "Minutes of the Cantors Ministers Cultural Organization, 1938–40," originally published in the *Journal of Synagogue Music;* to the Rabbinical Assembly of America for permission to reprint *"Beiti—Beit Tefillah"* and *"Shiru Lo,"* which originally appeared in *Conservative Judaism;* and to Rabbi Stuart Light for his felicitous English translations of the Hebrew found in those articles.

My appreciation, as well, to Rabbi Gordon Tucker for his help in clarifying the "woman's ordination" issue, and to Rabbi Raymond P. Scheindlin for reworking the translations and citations.

Janice Meyerson, who served as the editor of the manuscript, deserves my heartfelt gratitude for her support and thoroughness. Needless to say, errors in fact or editing which may still remain are mine alone.

C. D.

CONTENTS

Preface

Chapter 1: Antecedents (177?–1907)   1
* *Eighteenth-Century Hungary*   • *The Family Arrives and Is Dispersed*

Chapter 2: Childhood and Youth (1907–23)   5
* Beis Hamidrash *and the* Klauz   • *Budapest*   • *The Apprentice System*
* *Yeshiva*   • *Secularism Beckons*   • *Composition*   • *The* Aquatania
* *Welcome to America*

Chapter 3: First Stop: New York City (1923–28)   13
* *Scurry and Bustle*   • Hazzanim *Flock to America*   • *Study*   • *The Met*
* *Odd Jobs*   • *Recommendations*   • *Herzeliah*   • *Finding Music,*
WEVD, Hazzanim Farband   • *Cantorial Stars*   • *Modern Cantors Association*   • *Board of American Hazzan-Ministers*   • *First Job*

Chapter 4: Out of Lower Manhattan: College Point, Queens (1929–34)   25
* *Rabbi/Cantor*   • *Isaac Leeser and Mikveh Israel*   • *Solomon Schechter, Cyrus Adler, and the Jewish Theological Seminary of America*   • *Orthodox and Conservative Judaism*   • *Interviews—The* Probbeh-*Agents*

Chapter 5: On to Inwood (1935–41)   35
* *Mordecai Kaplan and the Seminary*   • *Schechter and Reform Leaders*
* *Choirs and Conductors*   • *Hazzanic Style*   • *Synagogue Music*
* *Kwartin*   • *The* Farband *and Its* Kibbetzarnyeh   • *Placement*
* *The AF of L*   • *Cantors Ministers Cultural Organization and Discovery of Minutes*

vii

Chapter 6: Northward Bound: Minneapolis (1941–45)   45
  • *Beth El*   • *Universal Jewish Encyclopedia*   • *Handball Champ*
  • *Hartford*

Chapter 7: A Brief Visit: Hartford (1945–46)   49
  • *Emanu El*   • *Nascent Stirrings: A Cantorial School*   • *Putterman*
  • *The Cantors Assembly of America*   • *Cantors Institute of the Seminary and College of Jewish Music Established*

Chapter 8: Philadelphia: First Encounter (1946–57)   55
  • *Beth El*   • *Encounters with Established Traditions*   • *President of Cantors Assembly*   • *Cantorial Training*   • *Seminary Music and Liturgy Faculty*   • *A Guiding Philosophy*   • *Regional Variations*   • *Eastern-Central-Western Europe*   • *Cantorial Curriculum*   • *Ramah*   • *What Made His Music Jewish?*

Chapter 9: On to Long Island: Malverne (1958–72); Long Beach (1972–78)   63
  • *Recitatives*   • *Retirement*   • *Substituting*

Chapter 10: Philadelphia: Second Time Around (1978–94)   67
  • *Gratz College*   • *Historic Vote: Women as Rabbis and as* Hazzanim
  • *The Synagogue Circuit*   • *Nathan Cummings Professor*   • *Honors and Reflections*   • *H. L. Miller Cantorial School of the Jewish Theological Seminary*   • Tam Venishlam

Notes   79

Bibliography of Max Wohlberg   81
  • *Biographical Article*   • *Articles on Jewish Music*   • *Critical Reviews*
  • *Essays*   • *Unpublished Articles*

Appendix A: Family Tree   99

Appendix B: Beiti—Beit Tefillah, by Max Wohlberg   101
  • *The Place*   • *The Atmosphere*   • *The* Siddur   • *The Congregation*
  • *Duration*   • *Language*   • Kavanah   • *The Cantor*   • Nusah
  • *Music*   • *The Composer*   • *Summary*

Appendix C: Shiru Lo, by Max Wohlberg   115
  • *Responses*   • *Congregational Song*   • *The Tunes*
  • *Recent Attempts*   • *Literature*   • *Analysis*   • *Texts*

Appendix D: Minutes of the Cantors Ministers Cultural Organization, 1938–40, by Max Wohlberg   125

Appendix E: Musical Autographs   147

PREFACE

For almost a half century, Max Wohlberg (1907–96) was well known in America and Israel as a *hazzan* (cantor officiating in a synagogue), composer, scholar, and teacher. He served as head of the *nusah hatefillah* (chant of prayers) department of the Cantors Institute of the Jewish Theological Seminary of America from the time of the Institute's founding in 1951, having begun his teaching career at the Seminary one year earlier. Through writings and lectures in English, Yiddish, and Hebrew, Wohlberg developed a scientific approach to *nusah hatefillah* and advocated research in a field famous for regionalization of materials. He helped to prepare generations of men and women to serve in the American cantorate, and his theoretical instruction was balanced by a rich treasury of humorous stories and insights.

Wohlberg was self-educated in the field of Jewish music. Born in Europe, he, like thousands of other boys, lived an orthodox life in a *shtetl* (small village) and grew up in the *yeshivot* (institutes of talmudic learning) of central Europe. Although it was apparent from an early age that he was musically gifted, he received no special training. His was not to be the usual route of youthful *meshorer* (apprentice choir singer); nor did he follow the path of some of his forebears, becoming a *hazzan-shohet* (cantor/ritual slaughterer). It was later in life and through his own efforts that he became an expert in the field of Jewish music and *hazzanut*. The story of how Wohlberg acquired the knowledge to eventually function as a practicing cantor in America without undergoing the common European route of apprenticeship to an established *hazzan* and prior to the establishment of cantorial schools in America gives the reader a fascinating insight into Wohlberg's determination to achieve professional success and the steps he took to ensure it.

During Wohlberg's early years in America, he was on close personal terms with such exceptional *hazzanim* as Yossele (Yosef) Rosenblatt (1882–1933), David Roitman (1884–1943), Gershon Sirota (1874–1943), Pierre Pinchik (c. 1900–1971), Mordechai Hershman (1888–1940), Moshe Koussevitsky (1899–1966), and Zavel Kwartin (1874–1953). They and others thrilled the newly arrived immigrant population and helped to keep alive the memories of the lives they had left behind. In the late twentieth century, Wohlberg was one of the few remaining *hazzanim* who were an integral part of early cantorial organizations such as the *Hazzanim Farband* (Cantors Association). His biography is important in a historical sense because it provides a reliable source for an understanding of that era. Wohlberg advocated changes in the musical service of the American synagogue, and he composed in a style that reflected this attitude. His philosophy, reflected in his articles and essays, touched upon every aspect of Jewish music.

The path that Wohlberg trod in his efforts on behalf of the Cantors Institute was similar to that blazed by an earlier Philadelphia hazzan, Sabato Morais (1823–97), who, with Alexander Kohut (1842–94), H. Pereira Mendes (1852–1937), and others, organized the Jewish Theological Seminary of America in 1887. They were preceded in their efforts to create a rabbinical school by Isaac Leeser (1806–68), also a Philadelphian and a Sephardic hazzan, who established Maimonides College in Philadelphia for that purpose in 1867. It is interesting to note that three Philadelphia hazzanim—Leeser, Morais, and Wohlberg—were intrinsically involved, each in his own way, in the Seminary and contributed to the evolution of Conservative Judaism in America.

Max Wohlberg successfully straddled four worlds—the Old and the New, the Jewish and the secular. A Hebraic scholar, he was also a man of the modern world, as at home in the tractates of the sages as he was in the philosophies of Western civilization. His odyssey from the Szatmar yeshiva in Hungary to the pluralistic society of America is engrossing and entertaining and will be enlightening for those who have an interest in *hazzanut,* in Jewish music, or in Judaica, as well as for the general reader who likes a good story.

As one born blind cannot understand the meaning of color, so the uninitiated cannot comprehend the power and the nobility of Hassidism. One who has not seen and been part of a S'udah Sh'lishit in an ever-deepening twilight with a group of fervent and pious Hassidim straining and bending forward toward the head of a long table in order to hear the softly and tenderly spoken words and anguished sighs of the rebbe, his words of soothing comfort and hopeful visions, one who has not joined in the fervent chant of the zemiros—such a person cannot conceive of an aliyat n'shamah, of losing all earthly bonds and of the rise of the purified soul in its desire to return to its heavenly source.

—Wohlberg, **Pirkei Hazzanut**, *The Cantors Voice* 6, no. 1 (October 1953)

1
ANTECEDENTS (177?–1907)

In the eighteenth century, Hungary became home to large numbers of Slovaks, Serbs, Rumanians, and Germans who had been encouraged to immigrate by the new Hapsburg rulers. Jews also joined the migration, increasing the Jewish population from approximately 20,000 to 80,000. Prior to the Holocaust, that number grew to more than 100,000. However, Jews from Galicia had already begun to cross the fertile valleys and dense forests of the Carpathian Mountains as early as 1684, as they fled the pogrom instigated by the Cossack leader Chmelnitski. For European Jewry fleeing continual pogroms, this formidable range, extending 900 miles between Czechoslovakia and Poland, became a tortuous, rocky path to freedom. Hungary, with its reputation as a place where Jews could survive in relative peace, became the destination for thousands of migrants of several distinct religious groups. Jews had lived in Hungary as far back as Roman times. Despite periods of persecution and suffering, the Jews of Hungary had always enjoyed a unique freedom of expression, envied by their long-suffering coreligionists in Galicia. The migration to Hungary increased even more in 1772, when Galicia was absorbed into the Austro-Hungarian Empire. The Galician Jews lived in much the same manner as their Ruthenian neighbors, whose customs and dress they adopted. The Carpathian Mountains were also the birthplace of Hassidism (a religious movement headed by a *tsaddik*, or "righteous man"), founded by Rabbi Israel ben Eliezer (1700–1760), known as the *Ba'al Shem Tov* (Master of the Good Name). To the simple folk, living frugal lives on tiny farms and in scattered villages, the idea of serving the Lord with joy and gladness was spiritually uplifting. The *Ba'al Shem Tov* taught that faith and prayer were as important as scholarship. To sing and dance in the service of the Almighty appealed as much to these simple folk as it was alien to those from the big cities who adhered stringently to more traditional prayer forms.

Ya'akov Wohlberg, Max's great-great-grandfather, joined the exodus into Hungary, arriving with his family and possessions in the latter half of the eighteenth century. His son Israel Shlomo became a *shohet* and settled near Tokay, where he had five sons and two daughters. The daughters married businessmen. Of the sons, the eldest, Leibish, became a *melamed* (teacher) and moved to Palestine; Kopel found work as a *shohet* and lived in Nagy Banya; Mendel emigrated to the United States and became a tailor; Yossele, Max's grandfather, married Roize, the daughter of a wealthy winegrower of Patroha; and Yehoshua, the youngest of the five boys, settled in the town of Arad, where he died of blood poisoning at an early age.

As a young boy, Yossele had been given four kreitzer by his father and sent to Krakow, where he enrolled in the yeshiva of Reb Shimon. After his studies were completed, Yossele returned home and married Roize, whose father was a *Hassid* (religious disciple) of the *rebbe* (common title given to a Hassidic leader) of Sanz. For a while the young couple lived in his house, until Yossele, restless and without a vocation, was taken by his father-in-law to the rebbe to ask his advice about Yossele's future. The rebbe suggested that he should become a *hazzan-shohet* because he was pious and could sing. The man who functioned as a cantor/ritual slaughterer was important to the Jewish communities of Eastern Europe because, while not greatly respected, the *hazzan-shohet* gave the community leadership in the prayer service as well as a supply of fresh meat for the table.

Yossele accepted the position of *hazzan-shohet* in the city of Ujhely, and Roize's father bought a house for the young couple. Some members of the community resented the fact that the young *shohet* and his wife, just starting their married life, had a home that was nicer than their own, and the ultra-pious disliked Yossele because of his modern dress and the fact that he read German newspapers. The couple, unhappy in Ujhely, looked to move elsewhere.

Hearing that the city of Szatmar needed a *hazzan-shohet*, Yossele went there, had a successful interview, and was assured that the job was his. However, the large contingent of Hassidim who were followers of the rebbe of

Sziget lived in Szatmar, and they decided that the young Yossele was too modern for their taste, and furthermore, he was a Hassid of the wrong rebbe; they wanted a *shohet* from their hometown of Sziget. These Hassidim managed to block the appointment with a writ from their rebbe. Yossele returned home disappointed but found a similar opening in Kisvarda, where he stayed and served the community until he died forty-five years later.

He and Roize were the parents of six sons and three daughters. The girls all married local merchants. Those of their children who survived the Holocaust settled either in the United States or in Israel. The eldest son, Boruch, was considered by the family to be somewhat of a renegade. After emigrating to the United States, he became a Reform rabbi. Another son, Kopel, suffered ill health and died at an early age. Yehoshuo Beirach owned a general store. He had been given a single name, Yehoshuo, when he was born; Beirach was later added to confuse the authorities when they made selections for the army. Asher reportedly had the most beautiful voice in the family and became *hazzan-shohet* in Hadhaz, where he raised ten children. Yirmiyohu (Jeremiah), the fifth son of Yossele and Roize, was Max's father. Yirmiyohu was a fine scholar, able to read and write in Hebrew, Yiddish, Hungarian, and German; he also had a voice of uncommon sweetness. The youngest of the sons was Avrohom Yitzchok, who became a professional *hazzan* holding positions in Budapest and in Brooklyn, New York.

Max's mother, Hermina, was a daughter of Zavel Mayer Wiszberger and his wife, who raised one son and eight daughters. After placing his son in a hardware business in Hrishev, Zavel Mayer sold his estate and moved his family to Homonna, where Hermina met and married Jeremiah Wohlberg.

Analyzing the synagogue music of Ashkenazic Europe, we are surprised at the comparatively few variations. . . . The explanation of this lies, I believe, in that: (1) there was strong attachment and strict adherence to traditional nusah; *(2) new melodies were applied mainly to the incidental and poetic sections of the prayer book, its structural core remaining untouched; (3) where a violation of proper mode was threatened, the new music was altered to fit into its frame; and (4) there was a liberal and friendly exchange of music among the traveling* hazzanim.

—Wohlberg, Pirkei Hazzanut, *The Cantors Voice* 1, no. 1 (May 1948)

2
CHILDHOOD AND YOUTH (1907–23)

Born Moshe ben Yirmiyohu on February 9, 1907, Miklos (Max) Wohlberg was the third child in the family; sister Blanka (Blanche) and brother Yitzchok Zvi (Harry) preceded him, and he was followed by brother Yosef (Joseph) and sister Madeline, who would be the child of Hermina's second marriage.

The family was supported by Hermina's father, Zavel Mayer, while Jeremiah spent his days studying. It was customary for wealthy fathers to seek out young scholars and rabbinical students as potential sons-in-law. The added prestige to the father-in-law through his daughter's marriage to a *lamdan* (scholar) was more than balanced by the financial support he gave them. For a short time, Jeremiah worked in a bank, but was far more comfortable with his books than with the world of commerce and soon returned to the patronage of his father-in-law. Zavel Mayer bought a small wine shop for Jeremiah, but Hermina did most of the work while her husband spent his time studying.

Weekday religious services in Homonna took place in the *beis hamidrash* (study house), and festival and High Holy Day services were conducted in the large and elaborate synagogue. The Hassidim prayed in their own enclave, a *klauz* (enclosed place). The synagogue had two floors, with seating for women on the upper level. The *beis hamidrash* was located in a separate building and, though almost as large as the synagogue, was more simply appointed. It was constructed on one level, its walls lined with books. A small section of the hall was designated for women.

Jeremiah prayed with the Hassidim in the *klauz* during the year. Because he had a beautiful voice, he was always asked to be the service leader in the *beis hamidrash* on the High Holy Days. Services in the larger synagogue were conducted by the community's professional cantor, Hazzan Malek. Jeremiah died of a heart attack in 1909 at the age of thirty-two, and Hermina assumed leadership of the family. Zavel Mayer closed the wine shop and arranged for her to operate a small grocery store, thinking that this was the best business for a widow with small children—even if the venture proved unsuccessful, the children would never go hungry. The grocery store did quite well under Hermina, but she found it difficult to give her children the attention they needed.

Hermina's sister Ilonka married Mordechai Stern, who owned Stern's Kosher Restaurant in Budapest. Aware of Hermina's circumstances, the childless Ilonka offered to take care of Max. Hermina agreed, and the four-year-old Max was sent to live with his aunt and uncle. Max's new lifestyle was very comfortable; he was the sole responsibility of a French maid who had been hired to watch over him. And it was in his uncle's restaurant that Max sang publicly for the first time. It became the custom on Friday evenings for little Miklos to stand on a table and entertain guests and family with *Shabbes zemiros* (songs appropriate for the Sabbath).

Max was registered in the all-day religious school of the Kazinczy Utca (Street) congregation. It was the largest orthodox synagogue in Budapest and had a fine *hazzan,* Jacob Hartman. There Max studied Mishnah (Oral Law) in Hungarian and in Hebrew. Because Stern's was a gathering place for the Jewish community, it was inevitable that Hartman should hear the young singer performing his repertoire of Sabbath songs, dressed in velvet with his small feet planted firmly on a restaurant tabletop. Impressed with the voice and poise of the boy, Hartman invited him to join the synagogue choir, conducted by a Mr. Gottlieb. Max sang in the alto section.

Budapest was a magnet for famous *hazzanim.* In the same section of town as Stern's Restaurant was the large Neolog (liberal) synagogue, known as the "Tabak Temple." Zavel Kwartin served there as *hazzan* before emigrating to America. The well-known Jacob Bachmann (1846–1905) sang in the large Rombach Temple of Budapest.

In 1915, a year after the outbreak of World War I, thousands of Hungarians fled into the interior of Hungary, where they hoped to escape the ravages of war. The cities of Ungvar, Munkacs, and Sziget were filled with refugees. Hermina packed up her family and their possessions and took to the crowded roads, seeking a safer haven in the interior. She and the children arrived in Budapest unharmed, where they were reunited not only with Max, but with Hermina's four remaining sisters as well.

In Budapest that same year, Hermina met and married Marcus Cohen, a widower with four children. Cohen was originally from the vicinity of Kraszna, and his children were about the same ages as the young Wohlbergs. After the wedding, the combined family left Budapest and moved to Sibiu, Transylvania, where daughter Madeline was born in 1917.

Their new stepfather decided that Harry and Max should be sent to study in the yeshiva at Kraszna, where Marcus had been born. The *Rosh Yeshiva* (head of the seminary) was Rabbi Yosef Mayer Eckstein. After an extended period there, the two boys were sent to continue their studies in the yeshiva at Nagy Karoly, where they were joined by brother Joseph and a stepbrother. When the boys were ready for more advanced learning, they were sent to the famous yeshiva in Szatmar, where the *Rosh Yeshiva* was Rabbi Leizer Yehudah Greenwald. Ironically, their father, Yirmiyohu, had been a student in the yeshiva of Sziget, and his sons studied in the rival yeshiva of Szatmar.

Max's voice had matured since his years in Budapest, and he enjoyed performing, expanding his repertoire to include songs in Yiddish and in Hungarian. Although he displayed obvious musical talent, Max had no opportunities in the *yeshivot* for formal music studies. Boys with vocal ability who were the sons of *hazzanim* studied with their fathers, or they might have been apprenticed to other *hazzanim* as *meshorerim* (singers) in their choirs. This apprentice system was the usual course for learning the cantorial craft.

Abba Weisgal (1885–1981), for example, who became *hazzan* of Chizuk Amuno Congregation in Baltimore, was the son of Shlomo Hayyim, who, after working as a day laborer and a haberdashery merchant, became *hazzanshohet* in Kikol, Poland. Abba sang in his father's choir and learned *nusah hatefillah*, but did not learn how to read music. The conditions surrounding Abba's music lessons, as described by Joseph Levine in "Emunat Abba," were delightfully casual and give insight into how some budding *hazzanim* learned their trade:

In 1895, at the age of ten, Abba was sent by his father, Shlomo Hayyim, to Shlomo's former teacher, Wolff Bendzel, also a *hazzan-shohet,* who lived in the town of Kavoul. In a system of barter, Bendzel had learned the skill of *shehitah* (ritual slaughtering) from Shlomo Hayyim, in return for his tutoring Shlomo in music. Now the son was sent to his father's teacher to learn sight-singing and to study theory. There between the stable stalls where *shehitah* was performed, Reb Wolff taught Abba to sight-read music and to count metered time.[1]

Max lived in the dormitory of the yeshiva, returning home twice each year, *bein hazmanim* (between the festive times). These visits coincided with the High Holy Days in the fall and Passover in the spring. Max usually welcomed these opportunities to leave the confines of the yeshiva, but because his relationship with Marcus Cohen was strained, Max sometimes avoided returning home for vacation. On those occasions, Max would visit his father's brother, Yehoshuo Beirach, who lived in Suleimed, which was near the Szatmar yeshiva and not far from the town of Zsibo. Max once arrived on the day before Purim, and his uncle greeted him with the news that the local *hazzan-shohet* was ill and unable to chant from the Scroll of Esther. "Are you able to read the Megillah [Scroll of Esther] for us?" he asked the fourteen-year-old. "Of course," Max replied instantly, realizing with some dismay a moment later that his response had been too quick. Separate melodic patterns exist for the chanting of the Pentateuch, the prophetic books, and the *megillot* (scrolls). Although Max knew the melodies of *Megillat Esther,* he had never chanted the scroll publicly. This impetuosity, coupled with a generous amount of chutzpah, would always be characteristic of Max, propelling him into situations that a more cautious individual would have avoided. Max got to work immediately, and that night chanted the scroll without pause or error.

On Purim, it was customary to leave plates on the floor before the Ark, into which congregants placed donations for the poor. One of the plates was set aside as a compensation for the Megillah reader. Because Max's uncle was in charge of the campaign to renovate the town's *mikveh* (ritual bath), he strongly advised that the lad donate the small sum that had been left for him to the synagogue. And so Max was denied his first professional compensation, which found its way into the *mikveh* fund of the town of Suleimed!

Max was a second-year student in the yeshiva, going with his class to the *Rosh Yeshiva* at the beginning of each week. The *Rosh Yeshiva* gave a *shiur* (lesson) to the boys, who were called *shiur geiers* (lesson-class goers). The first-year students were *bocherels* (young boys), too young for the *shiur*, and they were tutored by older boys, *hazor-bochers* (those who reviewed lessons for others). In this weekly *shiur*, the Rosh Yeshiva taught at length, referring to the commentaries. The students returned to their regular routine, and on Sundays, the rebbe would question them in a special oral examination at a *farheren* (hearing). Woe to the youngster who had not studied assiduously during the week and failed this public examination!

Max had become curious about the society and culture that existed beyond the yeshiva walls. He somehow secured novels, forbidden books, which he read in secret, starting with Dostoyevsky's *Crime and Punishment* and progressing to *The Brothers Karamazov*. A new world had opened up for him. He read Tolstoy's *War and Peace* and systematically went through Turgenev and Chekhov. In Hungarian translations he discovered de Maupassant, Flaubert, Zola, and Hugo, and read Conrad and Dickens. His interest in reading never stopped during his lifetime. In later years, he would regret only that his eyesight no longer permitted him to read as voraciously as he had in his youth.

In addition to reading "forbidden" literature, he became enamored of the theater. One evening, he managed to slip away from the yeshiva early, tucking his *peiyot* (traditional earlocks) behind his ears. He walked to the theater, bought a ticket, and saw his first play. He was soon hooked, often seeing several plays a week. The ushers grew to recognize him, and even when he bought a general admission ticket, he would be permitted to sit in a vacant, but more expensive, seat.

On one occasion, Max found a good seat in a box above the stage, but he was tired and fell asleep during the performance. When he woke up, the play was over, the audience gone, the doors locked, and the interior of the theater pitch-black. Frightened, he managed to climb down from the box to the stage and from there groped his way to a dressing room that faced the street. He opened a small window, crawled through it, and dropped to the ground below without breaking any bones. Making his way back to the yeshiva, he entered unobtrusively and mingled with the many boys who had stayed up late to study. On this occasion, as on many others, luck was with him.

Between his reading and his visits to the theater, he should have been ill-prepared for the rebbe's *farheren* sessions, but Max was able to cram a week's worth of studying into Thursdays and Fridays—no matter that he would forget by Monday what he had just committed to memory for Sunday. On the other hand, Max's elder brother, Harry, was a scholarly boy whose studies continued far into the night in preparation for the *farheren*. Harry, who in America would make significant contributions to traditional Jewish scholarship at Yeshiva University's Rabbi Yitzchak Elchanan Seminary, always knew the right answers, but it was Max, usually the first to raise his hand, who became the favorite of the *farheren* sessions.

On his trips back to Homonna, Max continued to ask Hazzan Malek to teach him how to read music, but the response was always the same: Malek was too busy. Declaring that he had no time to teach a *boychikel* (youngster), Malek sent the fifteen-year-old aspirant to a tenor singer of his choir, who, for a fee, tried to teach Max about music. It was only much later that Max realized that the tenor himself was not very knowledgeable. It would be years before Max had the time and the opportunity to educate himself musically.

Max's sister Blanka married Mord'che (Marcus) Eckstein, son of the same *Rosh Yeshiva,* Rabbi Yosef Mayer Eckstein, with whom the two Wohlberg boys had previously studied in Kraszna. Young Eckstein had come to Sibiu to work for Marcus Cohen in his building-materials business as bookkeeper/clerk-cum-manager and had fallen in love with Blanka. The two were married, and shortly after decided to emigrate to the United States.

Max's mother's marriage to Marcus Cohen was not a happy one. Her first husband, Jeremiah, had been a gentle and soft-spoken man; in contrast, Cohen was brusque and at times ill-mannered and moody. He liked the company of other men and enjoyed a glass of whiskey. Their marriage had been largely one of convenience: Cohen wanted a wife to run his house, and Hermina wanted security for herself and her children. But now, with Max and Harry in yeshiva and son-in-law Mord'che and daughter Blanka in America, Hermina found herself no longer able to live with Cohen. Leaving him, she and her two youngest children went to Budapest, where she found a small apartment. She stayed there for a short while, enrolling Joseph in a yeshiva. Several months later, Mord'che sent her boat tickets to America, she divorced Cohen and subsequently boarded ship with Joseph and Madeline.

Max was the next to leave. By 1923, the family had saved enough money to send the sixteen-year-old a second-class ticket on the Cunard Line for a ship departing from Cherbourg, France. Anxious to see his mother, brothers, and sisters, he left Hungary months before the ship's departure date. He traveled alone to Paris and then to Cherbourg, hoping to find a way to leave on an earlier ship. In a restaurant there, he heard Hungarian being spoken and unobtrusively attached himself to a family leaving that very day for America. Pretending to be one of their children, he trailed behind them up the gangplank of the luxury liner *Aquatania*. Max hid until the ship left harbor. Knowing that it would be impossible to return him to shore, he knocked on the purser's door, entered, and feigned confusion. "I don't know why I wasn't assigned a berth," Max petitioned in Hungarian, presenting the ticket that had been issued for a later departure and on a different ship. Persuasive even then, he talked himself into a room.

On board the ship, he wrote his first musical compositions: a setting of the four "Yehi Rotzon" (May it be Your will) prayers recited after the Torah readings on Monday and Thursday mornings; and a piece he called "Skalen an dem Mer" (Scales on the sea).

Ten days later, on a moonless Friday night, the *Aquatania* moved slowly past the Statue of Liberty. Max stood at the stern, watching the trail of bubbles disappear into the fog stretching back to his old life in Hungary. He carried with him the melodies of the Carpathian Mountains and of Budapest and the capacity to fuse the old with the new, the past with the future. The ship docked on New York's West Side, and all passengers were required to disembark. Despite the religious prohibition of doing so on the Sabbath, Max joined the others and left the ship.

His first thought in the New World was how to find his family. Max spied a Hassid, who had walked from the Lower East Side to meet an arriving relative. "Do you know where East Ninth Street off Avenue C might be?" Max queried in Yiddish. Max, the Hassid, and the Hassid's relative walked the entire width of lower Manhattan to the East Side. Max found the building where his mother, brothers, and sisters lived, climbed the stairs to their apartment, and knocked on the door. He heard his mother's voice call out, "I'll bet it's a telegram from Moishe." Opening the door, she was confronted by a beaming Max, who said simply, "*Dos bin ich alein*" (It's only me) before embracing her. He had arrived in the New World!

The first Hassidim, we are told in the Mishnah, spent an hour before prayer in order to achieve a mood of devotion. Properly, they looked on prayer as a great spiritual adventure, requiring adequate preparation and concentration. They realized that it is almost impossible to transport oneself from a commonplace and mundane atmosphere into one of holy awe without a period of transition. They also sensed that one ought to shake off the dust of the road before approaching the throne of the Almighty. The need for attunement with the spirit of the synagogue liturgy before praying is a need seldom realized in our own day. Because we all too often fail to achieve the full measure of emotional satisfaction from our prayers, and because considerations of time have acquired a quality of such urgency, it is difficult to assume attitudes of contemplation, meditation, introspection, and devotion.

Hurriedly we rush into our prayers and breathlessly we gallop through them, always keeping an eye on the relentlessly moving hands of the clock. Is it any wonder that we miss the warmth and the fervor that accompanied the prayers of old? How much inspiration can be derived by a worshiper who darts into the synagogue in the middle of the service, worried about parking problems, and remains in the rear of the sanctuary so that he can rush out at a predetermined time, irrespective of the point in the service?

To be among the first to arrive for prayers and among the last ten to leave was a distinction highly valued in days gone by. Would it not serve as a fine example for our congregations if the first to arrive at services would find the rabbi and the cantor at their places, reciting, mezza voce, *the* Birkhot Hashahar? *Some of the beautiful prayers that fell victim to recent editorial deletion could be reintroduced here and chanted at leisure. If, as it seems, we cannot delay ending the service beyond a given time, perhaps we can advance its beginning and so afford those who wish a more perfect communion with their Maker an opportunity to enter into it gradually and more fully.*

—**Wohlberg, Pirkei Hazzanut,** The Cantors Voice 9, no. 2 (February 1958)

3
FIRST STOP: NEW YORK CITY (1923–28)

The great migration from Eastern Europe, which began in the 1870s, radically altered the life of New York Jewry. A million Yiddish-speaking displaced Jews settled in the city. Mostly from Eastern Europe, they were poor and accustomed to hard work and struggle for survival. Unlike the more cultured, economically secure, and Americanized Jews who lived uptown, they were referred to as the alien and plebeian "Russian" or "downtown" Jews. The Wohlbergs, with limited means and living in an apartment on Ninth Street in lower Manhattan, were definitely in the latter category.

In those first days in America, Max was full of the drive and energy typical of that immigrant generation. The sign boards were in English and Yiddish, some of them in Russian. The scurry and bustle of the people were overwhelmingly greater, both in volume and intensity, than in his native town. Indeed, the atmosphere was of another sort. The swing and step of the pedestrians, the voices and manner of the street peddlers, and a hundred and one other things seemed to testify to far more self-confidence and energy, to larger ambitions and wider scopes, than the streets and byways of Hungary.

Soon Max was in the center of that scene as he negotiated the crowded downtown streets behind a pushcart filled with cans of paint. He became as familiar with the byways of lower Manhattan as he had been with the rutted paths of Homonna. He also sold spark plugs and grease fittings, making his sales pitch in Hungarian, German, or Yiddish, as the occasion required. For a short time, he worked in a tenement factory, sewing neckties. Many immigrants without specific skills followed this route, working odd jobs for short periods of time while looking for their niche in the New World.

Max owed his brother-in-law, Marcus Eckstein, a debt of gratitude, for it was he who guided him toward the cantorate. Convinced that Max could capitalize on his vocal ability, Eckstein brought him to a small synagogue on Avenue C in Manhattan. Max was introduced to the members of Etz Chayim (Tree of Life) as a young singer and former yeshiva student who was interested in becoming a *hazzan*. Max sang for them and was invited to lead services for a Sabbath. The congregation advertised the event and sold tickets. Max's first performance as a cantor was financially successful for the synagogue but not for himself. He would later learn to "strike a deal" before—and not after—he sang.

Many congregations in New York relied on this system in order to supplement their budgets. Joseph Levine records that extravagant advertisements were the order of the day, as this article from the Yiddish newspaper *Morgen Zhurnal* (Morning Journal) of July 5, 1920, makes clear:

> **Wonderful Young Hazzan Arrives on the Kaiserin Augusta Victoria and Will Make His First Appearance This Sabbath**
>
> Hazzan Herman Semiatin is a young man about thirty-five years old. His heroic tenor voice and great talent have brought him renown throughout Poland and England. He is blessed with one of the most wonderful voices a *hazzan* ever had: huge, thunderous, yet with a uniform golden quality that is sweetly appealing. He is a classic chanter of the prayers and, in Europe, had a reputation as the forger of a new path in *nusah* that was strongly accepted by the cognoscenti.[2]

Because Max realized that his musical background was limited, he embarked on a calculated course of study, determined to understand the mechanics of music. He purchased a piano from a synagogue that held services in a converted movie theater. The piano, a baby grand, had been in use during the building's movie days when it had been played for silent films. It was transported to the Wohlbergs' Lower East Side apartment building, where it was hoisted through the window into the living room.

> The arrival of the piano was a major event on our block. Because of its size, it could not be maneuvered around the stairs. It thus had to be hoisted with pulleys from the roof. When it was parallel with our floor, it was found to be too wide to go into the window. Then the window frames were removed, and, accompanied by unholy oaths, it was eased into the apartment. As its shape was oblong and its top was flat, it served as an extra bed in emergencies. I clearly recall that the piano with its moving cost me twenty-five dollars. My mother insisted that I give the movers a two-dollar tip. She, God bless her soul, was always extravagant. When years later, we moved, we left the piano for the next tenants.³

Because Max had no knowledge of sight-singing, could not read musical notation, and could not play the piano, he spent long hours at the keyboard, picking out the notes, trying to learn the major and minor scales. He relied upon his ear to distinguish between half-steps and whole steps, playing them one note at a time and then writing down the scales and memorizing them. He bought a book that explained sight-singing, and for months, yeshiva-style, he studied late into the night until he had mastered all the exercises. Max then sought more specialized instruction from Arnold Powell:

> Powell was the son of Hazzan Zemachson and a first-rate musician, known to be a highly eccentric and outspoken individual. Some of his compositions were performed by the New York Philharmonic under Stokowski. After a few sessions with me, he candidly announced that in his opinion I'd never amount to much.⁴

Powell was recommended to Max by Henry Lefkowitz, the owner of the Metro Music Company, which, at the time, was the publisher and largest seller of Jewish music in New York. Second Avenue show tunes and cantorial recitatives found equal space on its shelves. "Metro" had been established by Joseph Katz, who, in addition to being a publisher, was a singer who conducted, leading choirs for the High Holy Days. Lefkowitz also conducted choirs for the High Holy Days and purchased Metro Music, moving it into a building at Second Avenue and Fourth Street, where it became a familiar landmark. Lefkowitz was well acquainted with Powell and, knowing the sorry state of his finances, often supplied him with free music paper.

Lessons between the young man and the impecunious music teacher proved to be a fair exchange; in spite of his conviction that Max would never amount to much musically, Powell helped his pupil learn about music and Max added to the meager income of his teacher.

> I had an irrepressible urge to study. I tried to read every book, pamphlet, and article that had the remotest relation to the subjects of Jewish music and liturgy. Every free moment was spent in the music sections of public libraries in Manhattan, as well as the one at the Jewish Theological Seminary. I believe I went through every item in their catalogs with relevance to my subjects. English, German, Hebrew, and Yiddish offered no problems. Articles in French I had translated into English for better comprehension. Alas, there was very little of this literature in my mother tongue, Hungarian.[5]

During this time, Hermina managed to save a modest sum of money and opened a small restaurant on Avenue B near Eighth Street. She was a good cook, and the restaurant attracted a small clientele appreciative of her Hungarian cuisine. While there may have been other reasons for its closing, Max seemed convinced that the failure of the business was due to Hermina's serving the same bountiful portions to her customers as she gave to her children at home.

Max applied to the Metropolitan Opera for a position in its chorus. Unaccustomed to auditions, Max was asked to sing scales by a Mr. Petri. When the range became too high for him to sing comfortably, the young singer switched to the lower octave. "Continue, continue!" demanded Petri of a Max who declined to "strain his voice." Needless to say, he was not accepted. Not to be denied, Max re-auditioned the following year. He now knew what to expect! Petri only wanted to see how high he could sing. This time, he gained a position as a tenor in the chorus and held it for two seasons.

Max's voice was relatively small but was extremely expressive and capable of fine nuance. As with many *hazzanim* who chose to live as congregational *klei kodesh* (religious officials), the lack of great vocal volume was not a handicap in his securing synagogue positions. Max studied voice with a Russian singer, Boris Skwartzoff (Starling), and later with Walter Mattern. Through Skwartzoff, Max became acquainted with vocal literature, particularly Russian art songs. Max was a good student of language, so when he happened to sing some songs in Russian at a gathering of Russian expatriates, he was approached by members of the group, speaking to him in Russian. He confessed that he was not able to speak the language but thanked them for their compliments on his pronunciation.

During the 1920s, Max continued to work at a variety of jobs while English studies occupied him at night school. For a time, he was employed at the Horowitz-Margareten matzo bakery on Fourth Street and Avenue D, where he packed matzo into boxes. He was paid eighteen dollars a week and often spent long hours working overtime. In one memorable week prior to Passover, he worked feverishly during the day, slept for a few hours at the factory during the night before starting to work again, and earned fifty-four dollars in overtime payments.

Max also worked in a small factory making wooden picture frames, always singing at his work table. The boss soon found that when Max sang a sprightly melody, he could be counted on to work quickly, and when he sang a slow tune, he worked in its tempo. "Sing a march, Max!" was often his command as he made the rounds of his shop. He also clerked in a dry-goods store near his apartment. Because Max was quick and helpful to customers and the proprietor was never in the store, neighbors assumed that he owned the shop. After working there for several months, he was awakened by cries of "Wake up, your store is on fire!" as indeed, it was. A fire of suspicious origin had finished his career in the dry-goods business. This was followed by a short stint as a pressing-machine operator in a suit factory. There he pressed the inner linings of suit jackets. Short in stature and very slight, he had to jump on the foot pedal of the pressing machine in order to close it.

Max finished night school and decided that he wanted to be a teacher. He had just turned nineteen and enrolled as a full-time student at the Herzeliah Teachers Seminary in Manhattan but, impatient and with money needed at home, he soon left, looking for work. He turned to his brother-in-law, Marcus Eckstein, for advice. Eckstein recommended Max to a friend, a Mr. Phillips, who was principal of Yeshiva Ohel Torah on New York's East Side. Phillips accepted him as a substitute teacher. Patient and methodical, Max proved to be a natural and effective teacher in spite of his youth.

During the week, while making his rounds of the school, Phillips passed the closed door of Max's classroom. He heard no noise from a class well known to be raucous and hard to control. Phillips quietly opened the door, half expecting to see the young substitute teacher prostrate on the floor, at the mercy of boys twice his size. He was surprised at the sight of the diminutive and quiet-spoken Max, perched on his stool, surrounded by a circle of boys, listening to his stories of the "Old Country." Seeing that Max had the situation well under control, Phillips closed the door behind him,

Max continued to sing in the community and gained a reputation as a fine young *hazzan*. He was invited by various neighborhood congregations to lead Sabbath services. Leading services without remuneration in the hope of landing a job was typical of the times.

> I received invitations from a few small synagogues to chant the Sabbath service, mostly without remuneration. One of these, Etz Chayim on Avenue C, actually had tickets printed for my *davening* on Shavuot in 1926. As my idealistic brother-in-law assured the congregation that I would not accept money from his *shul*, I was presented with a fine letter and large woolen *tallis*.[6]
>
> The very method by which cantors were selected by congregations was degrading. Week in, week out, cantors were asked to compete with one another, granting free concerts to the congregation on each successive Sabbath.[7]

Max had sung several times at a synagogue on Lewis Street on the Lower East Side, and he knew that the congregation was searching for a *hazzan* for the High Holy Days. They called Max and asked him to come to the synagogue to audition for the job. "But why must I come again?" Max asked. "You know my voice. It hasn't improved since you last heard me." "You'll have to come again so that the whole congregation can hear you," was the reply. Max dutifully went to Lewis Street and sang selection after selection to much applause. "*Noch eppes . . . zing noch eppes* [more . . . sing more]," they called out. Max finally felt that enough was enough and asked for a decision. The older members of the congregation replied that they had indeed enjoyed his singing but that he was too young for the position. He had made the trip for nothing. "In spite of my fine *davening*, they thought it would be unseemly for a congregation including numerous venerable gentlemen to be led in High Holy Day prayers by a young boy."[8]

A distant cousin invited Max to lead services in his synagogue in Borough Park, Brooklyn, with the promise of payment. Max complied, and the members seemed pleased. On the following day, the cousin handed Max about seventy dollars, his first compensation for singing. His luck had changed!

Shortly thereafter, Max was hired as a tenor in the choir of Cantor Levy of the "Glenmore and Miller Avenue" synagogue in the Brownsville section of Brooklyn. How he got there gives insight into the system of referrals common to the cantorial network in those times. Max's uncle Avrohom Yitzchok Wohlberg, who had been a *hazzan* in Budapest, emigrated to America and found a position in Brooklyn, where he became friendly with his colleagues in the cantorial community. When Max inquired about work for the High Holy Days, his uncle passed him on to Cantor Jacob Schraeter, whom he knew as a good *hazzan* with contacts and who was also a mentsch.

> My visit to the Schraeter home was as delightful as it was successful. But a word must be said about the Schraeter family. Jacob was a good, matter-of-fact, practical, no-nonsense *hazzan* and *mohel*. He and his dear wife were warm and friendly, qualities often found in Jewish homes. What was unusual about the family was the extent of the role of music in its life. The two youngsters I saw there at play grew up to be colleagues Alvin and Arnold. A brother of Jacob was Henry Schraeter, a well-known cantor and voice teacher. He was the first teacher of Leonard Warren, and his wife was the renowned dramatic soprano Viola Philo, who appeared at the Metropolitan Opera and became a perennial star at Roxy's and at Radio City. Cantor Schraeter asked me to sing for him. If my recollection is correct, I sang a passage from the weekday *Amidah* [core of the daily blessings]. His comment, I recall clearly, was concise: There were too many "ideas" I tried to put across. My singing should not be too involved and cluttered with too many elements. I should rather strive for simplicity and clarity. This was, I know, excellent advice that, alas, I did not always heed.[9]

Schraeter, in turn, passed Max's name on to Dr. Edward Rappaport, a local dentist. Rappaport was Schraeter's nephew and Cantor Levy's choir conductor. It was through such an intricate system of referrals that many Jewish singers found work. By this time, Max was able to read music and was welcomed by Rappaport as a useful addition to the choir. Max attended rehearsals dutifully and sang with the choir on the first day of Rosh Hashanah.

> As only a few compositions involved the cantor and since the members of the choir knew their music, rehearsals were few and pleasant. The fair-size choir stood surrounding the pulpit, facing the conductor and behind him the cantor. The first day of Rosh Hashanah passed uneventfully. On the second day, as soon as the *hazzan* began the *Hineni* ["Poor in worthy deeds, I am frightened in thy

presence. . . . I have come to plead before thee on behalf of thy people Israel," the opening and personal prayer of the *hazzan*], he slumped to the floor and pandemonium broke loose. After some confusion, it became clear that he had suffered a heart attack. He was placed in a taxi and driven home. The rabbi of the congregation was Goodblatt, a revered elderly gentleman. He was the father of Rabbi Goodblatt of Beth Am in Philadelphia. As soon as the event occurred, he approached the pulpit asking the congregation to remain calm.[10]

Goodblatt and the president of the congregation held a quick meeting with Rappaport, the choir conductor: "This new young boy in the choir seems to know what it's all about. I wouldn't be surprised if he could finish the service." They approached Max, who stood with the other choir members in a semi-circle around the *shulhan* (reading table). "Can you finish the service?" they inquired. "Of course," was his quick reply.

> With the confidence of youth, I launched into the service, sang the solos, improvised and acted as if I did this every other week. With a sigh of relief, the rabbi soon returned to his place and I, encouraged by the evident satisfaction of the choir leader and congregation, concluded the service. No sooner did I sing the last *omen* when the president embraced me—my face against his diaphragm—and exclaimed: "*Oi, far vos hot yener noch nechten nit gechalesh* [Why couldn't the other one have fainted yesterday]?" As the *hazzan* was not well enough for Yom Kippur, I again replaced him. Thus did I make my debut in Brownsville.[11]

After the High Holy Days, Max thought of finding his own pulpit, but was not yet ready to commit himself to a full-time position. After a year of study, he secured a place for himself at the "Gates Avenue" shul in Brooklyn. Again, a system of referrals made this possible. This time it was through Herman Wohlberg, his eldest cousin, who was a member there. Max was required to train a choir, and he recruited his brother Joseph, two nephews, and three other boys.

> In 1927, I accepted the High Holy Day position at Agudas Achim on Gates Avenue in Brooklyn. The synagogue was in a renovated movie theater. My fee was $900 or $950. However, for this magnificent sum, I was also to furnish a choir. Since my octet included my younger brother and two of my nephews, I managed to clear approximately $700.[12]

Looking for music for his choir, he turned to Cantor Schraeter for help:

> I had accepted the offer with alacrity, without realizing that I did not have an appropriate choral repertoire. Jacob Schraeter, without a moment's hesitation, provided me with a complete repertoire in simple arrangement. The performance of my choir was less than modest; however, the congregation retained my services for all the festivals and special Sabbaths of the year. I thus completed my apprenticeship and began to build my music library.[14]

Schraeter had given Wohlberg two-part music, arranged for tenor and bass. Two-part vocal music supporting the *hazzan* was part of the synagogue tradition, dating back to the late seventeenth and early eighteenth centuries, when, as musicologist Abraham Zvi Idelsohn has described:

> *hazzanim* . . . often brought with them a choir . . . singer [*singerel,* a young boy with a high voice] and bass who stood at either side . . . [singing] by ear alone, improvising rather than following a prearranged harmony.[11]

Max was invited to lead some services at the Young Israel synagogue on Bedford Avenue in the Williamsburg section of Brooklyn. He also began singing on radio station WEVD's *Synagogue Music* program, sponsored by Maxwell House Coffee. Many New York–based *hazzanim* of the time also participated as solo singers. That they were also part of the sponsors' product advertising is recalled by Mark Slobin in a reprint from the *Morgen Zhurnal* of September 5, 1940:

> **What Famous New York Cantors Say about Maxwell House Coffee:**
> "After vacation I am happy that I can again enjoy the richer, better Maxwell House Coffee regularly." In thousands of Jewish homes, [families] . . . feel again the same thrill as Cantor Roitman and other well-known cantors—the enjoyment of the coffee that they had been missing . . . with milk or cream for breakfast and black after a *fleyshige* meal. *Gut bisn letstn tropn* [good to the last drop].[15]

Max decided that it was time to find a full-time position and turned to the *Hazzanim Farband* (cantorial organization) for placement. The *Farband* was originally a club of a dozen or so of the most prominent New York *hazzanim,* who had banded together to help indigent colleagues. The *Farband* was founded in 1897, incorporated in 1919, and later developed into the Jewish Ministers Cantors' Association of America. Many retired or unemployed *hazzanim* of the time, such as the old and embittered Zeidel Rovner (né Jacob Samuel Marogowsky, 1856–1943), were in dire straits. Rovner, a masterful conductor and composer of liturgical music, ended his days in a poorly furnished tenement apartment impoverished and ill. Max and others visited him often to offer support but alas, their support did not include funds from the *Farband*, which were most often in short supply.

The degree of the *Farband*'s success is disputed. Some ex-members felt that it was never more than a patronage club and that it compromised itself by taking part-time cantors and not exclusively full-time professionals. Discussing the *Farband* years later, Max said:

> During the thirties, the preponderant number [of *hazzanim*] in New York and its environs were members of the *Farband*. Unfortunately, the *Farband* saw fit to open its ranks to even such as were but remotely related to *hazzanut*, so long as they were willing to pay dues. As a result, our colleagues included *shamashim* [sextons], *shochtim* [slaughterers], *melamdim* [Hebrew teachers], *mashgichim* [supervisors of kosher food], *mohelim* [circumcisors], kosher-delicatessen clerks, and whoever functioned or aspired to function as a *hazzan* for as few as three days a year.[16]

Meetings were not only devoted to business but also provided ample opportunities for friendly talk and gossip. The *Farband*'s membership included such famous *hazzanim* as Yosef Rosenblatt, Zavel Kwartin, Mordechai Hershman, David Roitman, Leib Glantz (1898–1964), Pierre Pinchik, Joshua Samuel Weisser (1888–1952), and Adolph Katchko (1896–1958). While Reform cantors also belonged to the *Farband*, they had their own organization, known as the Modern Cantors Association and later as the Board of American Hazzan-Ministers, headed by longtime president Walter Davidson (1903–89) from 1928 to 1953. In 1934, in an effort to establish its position in Reform congregations, the organization published *The Ministerial Status of the Cantor: A Collection of Facts Upholding the Cantorial Right in Religious Functions*.

At the *Farband*, Max met Rosenblatt, who invited him to sing at a Hanukkah concert at his synagogue, Ohev Tzedek, in Harlem on 116th Street. It was an important occasion for the youthful Max, just beginning his career, and he wanted to make a good impression. He wrote a special composition for himself to sing and purposefully chose the text "Zoreia Tzedokos" (Sowing righteousness), knowing that Rosenblatt had already recorded his own, very well known, "Zoreia Tzedokos" several years earlier. With his customary chutzpah, Max wanted to effect a coup to display that he was a composer as well as a cantor. He wrote a flashy recitative that required him to sing from his lowest note to his highest.

On the fateful evening, he stepped up to the *bimah*, which was enclosed by a low iron railing. Max caught the steady gaze of the bearded and world-famous Rosenblatt and became so flustered that he couldn't find his pitch when he struck his tuning fork. He continued to hit the instrument against the railing until he "thought it would break." Without the right pitch, he threw caution to the wind and began to sing, but much higher than he had intended. Thus, he couldn't reach the high notes he had written, and his improvisation did not work out. As an embarrassed Max was leaving the *bimah* he passed Rosenblatt, who shook his hand and commiserated, *"Ich farshtei* [I understand]." Max later advised his students that "the best improvisation is written out in advance."

The Hanukkah fiasco behind him, and again in good spirits, Max inquired at the *Farband* about a job. There was an inquiry from a congregation in College Point, Queens, he was told. He auditioned for the position and was accepted by Congregation Ahavas Achim. At last, he had a real job. He felt that he was on his way!

As the system of cantillation is a primary example of the musical genius of the Jew, so is the recitative the perfect vehicle for the music of the synagogue. There is one paramount requirement in synagogue music, and that is nusah. *Generations of worshipers have molded the expressions of their deepest supplications and chief joys in age-old modes and in hallowed* nusah. *This has been a field of contention between our more recent synagogue composers and our traditionalists.*

—Wohlberg, Pirkei Hazzanut, *The Cantors Voice* 5, no. 2
(December 1952)

4
OUT OF LOWER MANHATTAN: COLLEGE POINT, QUEENS (1929–34)

College Point's Congregation Ahavas Achim had sought one man for the combined position of rabbi/*hazzan*, and although Max had been looking only for a cantorial position, he became the religious head of the congregation as well. This dual function was not unlike the service rendered to early American congregations by the first *hazzan*-ministers in the New World, who "read" the service as well as preached. Early American Jewish clergy were, in fact, *hazzanim*. Until the 1840s, no ordained rabbi lived and worked in the United States. The *hazzan* was the chief religious leader, who acted as reader at services, conducted weddings and funerals, and was recognized by the non-Jewish community as the "minister" of the synagogue. He circumcised the male children, taught them in a makeshift school, and prepared them for bar mitzvah. He often acted as the communal *shohet,* he married and buried, chanted the services, and augmented his meager income by engaging in trading or language instruction. The *hazzan* was also called upon to represent the Jewish community by making public formal addresses.

However, in contrast to the norm, Mikveh Israel in Philadelphia gave the mandate of leading the congregation in prayer as prime synagogal function to American-born *hazzan* Gershom Mendes Seixas (1746–1816). The congregation also designated two or three additional staff members (rabbi, *shohet,* and *shamash*) in its 1798 constitution. The rabbi was the teacher of the young, the *shohet* was the ritual slaughterer who supplied the community with kosher food used according to Jewish dietary laws, and the *shamash* was the caretaker of the synagogue and its ritual objects and a general factotum.

In 1828 or 1829, Sephardic Mikveh Israel turned to Isaac Leeser, a young Ashkenazic Jew newly arrived from Germany, to assume the position of *hazzan*. Talented and industrious, he had attracted the congregation's attention with an essay he had written in defense of Judaism in 1825. He eventually became a national figure as editor, educator, and journalist, and made important contributions to American Judaism. He founded *The Occident*, the first successful American Jewish newspaper, published many textbooks for children, established the Jewish Publication Society of America, and translated the Bible into English. He favored changes in synagogue ritual that did not impinge on traditional theology.

Leeser's successor as *hazzan* in Philadelphia's Congregation Mikveh Israel, Sabato Morais, served the congregation for forty-seven years, until his death in 1897. He had a love for Jewish music and a respect for the service. Morais founded the Jewish Theological Seminary in 1887, and his enthusiasm helped place the Seminary on a sound footing at a time when American Jewry was drifting toward the Reform. Morais struggled to combine the Sephardic and Ashkenazic elements in his own community and influenced many who became leaders of American Jewry. Regarding Morais and Wohlberg, both founders of Jewish educational institutions at the Seminary, Joseph Levine comments:

> [They] were players in American Jewry's late-nineteenth- and late-twentieth-century searches for an authentic Judaism of its own. Morais was willing to forgo his native Sephardic *minhag* and helped create a simpler prayer book that all America could use and thereby "effectively stop capricious changes." In this, he presaged Wohlberg's plea (years later) for a "common mode of worship in the American synagogue." Both had important organizational skills and ably selected a strong faculty. Both personified the Americanization process at its best by attempting to strengthen traditional practice through creative renewal. . . . Both Wohlberg and Morais journeyed weekly from Philadelphia to New York in obvious respect for their congregational commitments.[17]

Morais was representative of an established American Sephardic Jewish community, unlike those Jews pouring into the United States from all parts of Eastern Europe. The great tide of their immigration began in 1882 and would create complex problems, already recognized by a nascent Jewish Theological Seminary.

Solomon Schechter (1847–1915), rabbinic scholar and traditionalist, after establishing his career as discoverer of the Cairo geniza, assumed his position as president of the Jewish Theological Seminary of America in 1902. The course he plotted for the Seminary was one of traditional Judaism and a devotion to the scientific study of that tradition. As the main architect of Conservative Judaism, he attracted a distinguished faculty and saw the Seminary become an important center for Jewish learning and intellectual revival. His writings and addresses are indispensable to an understanding of the Conservative movement.

Schechter proposed that, under his guidance, the Seminary would become a link for the new immigrants between their European past and their new lives in America. However, among the many problems that they faced was that the effort to establish themselves economically did not give the new immigrants enough time to support institutions such as the Seminary.

Cyrus Adler (1863–1940), scholar, teacher, editor, and traditionalist, was also respected in government and financial circles. He was responsible for securing financial support for the Seminary and its faculty and had the ability to persuade men of means to provide for an institution that would be able to satisfy the needs of the flood of traditional-minded Jews now entering the New World. He was executive administrator of the Seminary, and when Schechter died in 1915 he became president.

The Wohlbergs, part of that influx of Jewry from Eastern Europe, were unaware of the Seminary and untouched by its influence. By 1929, the family had moved out of Manhattan and into the Williamsburg section of Brooklyn. The fall of the stock market in October 1929 and the ensuing Great Depression weighed heavily upon Jewish life and caused many small congregations to find ways to economize. The Jewish community, which had erected elaborate synagogues, Jewish hospitals, and orphanages during prosperity, frequently assuming heavy mortgages, now could neither maintain them nor even retain them. Emergency measures had to be taken; budgets were reduced and rabbis discharged.

Congregation Ahavas Achim in College Point found itself in such a predicament; unable to afford a "real" rabbi but nevertheless determined to survive the economic blight that covered America, they were looking for a *kol bo* (many-dutied functionary) to keep them afloat. Somehow Max found out about the opening, applied, and was accepted. At Ahavas Achim, Max was required to prepare sermons and to attend to pastoral duties. Drawing upon a knowledge of biblical exegesis acquired during his yeshiva days, Max prepared weekly sermons that he wrote out in full. These sermons in English were a challenge to him. His English had greatly improved since his days as a sparkplug salesman, but his delivery was somewhat halting and he often mispronounced words. Both Max and the congregation lived through his running battle with the language, and in his later lectures and speaking engagements he was admired as a polished and precise speaker.

Max obtained a license from the State of New York that enabled him to perform weddings for congregants. In addition to leading services and delivering sermons, he taught in the congregational religious school. He was also required to read the Torah and sound the shofar on the High Holy Days. Regarding these duties at College Point, he later joked that he was relieved not to have to "sweep up the place" as well.

Over the Sabbath, he stayed in College Point with the family of Bruno Slansky and was able to walk to the synagogue for services, in keeping with the prohibition against driving on the Sabbath. In order to commute from Brooklyn to Ahavas Achim for his duties during the week, Max bought his first automobile, a Chevrolet, for $850. His first week of ownership, while driving from the dealer to his home in Williamsburg, he turned his head to look back at a street sign and hit a lamppost. The car was wrecked but Max was unhurt and afterward became an exemplary driver, aware that "an automobile is not designed to work on automatic pilot."

Max found the rabbinic aspects of his dual position satisfying and, for a time, considered becoming a rabbi. He and his brother Harry had been raised in an observant family and had been educated in *yeshivot* in Europe, so the rabbinate would have been a natural course for both of them. Harry had already decided to become a rabbi, but Max thought that his religious views had become too liberal for a rabbi who would function in a traditional congregation. Instead of becoming a seminarian, he returned to his Jewish studies at the Herzeliah Teachers Seminary. He left behind the dogmatic orthodoxy of his youth and became associated with Conservative Judaism.

Max maintained a program of study that continued throughout his life, as intense and steadfast as it had been in the yeshiva. Through hard work, he acquired an extensive English vocabulary and was able to express himself well. In the same manner, he set himself the task of becoming an expert in Jewish music. He methodically read through the Mishnah and Gemara (Jewish code of laws and its elaboration) references to music, then went on to study all the journals and books on Jewish music that he could find. His copious notes formed the basis of future lectures and articles for which he became well known. Max's early days in New York were spread thin with a plethora of short-lived, nonmusical jobs; in contrast, his first full-time position gave him the time and perspective to focus specifically on his subject. In addition, his five years of sermonizing at Ahavas Achim contributed to his future success as lecturer and teacher.

He also began an intensive study of cantorial recitatives, particularly those written in the elaborate Eastern European manner. Max had an excellent ear as well as a retentive memory and analyzed recitatives by transcribing them from recordings. He was particularly fond of the works of Joshua Weisser (né Joshua Samuel Pilderwasser). Max's early compositions for solo voice ("Av Horahamim," 1930; "Mi Shebeirach," 1930; "Shoshanas Ya'akov," 1934) follow the florid style embodied in Weisser's compositions. His preoccupation with the recitative was undoubtedly a result of his own requirements at the pulpit. The absence of choral titles among his *oeuvre* of this period might be due to the fact that there was no choral program at Ahavas Achim, so he had no impetus to write choral music. Armed with natural musical ability, he would later create a large number of solo recitatives and a modest compilation of choral works. As a melodist without formal training, he found it easier to write for unaccompanied *hazzan* than for more complex forces.

Some synagogue composers did have solid musical training. Alexander Ersler (1854–1923), for example, sang as a *meshorer* in the choirs of two *hazzanim* and learned sight-singing as well as harmony and composition. Ersler's teachers were the composers Hirsch Weintraub (1811–82) and Louis Lewandowski (1821–94). The latter's music was easy to perform and had great appeal. Lewandowski achieved widespread popularity not only in Europe but in the United States as well. A weak and sickly youth who was taken under the wing of a cousin of Mendelssohn, Lewandowski became a formidable presence in synagogue music.

Max became fast friends with Cantor Meier Koerner of Scranton, Pennsylvania, whom he had met at meetings of the *Farband.* In Europe, it was quite common for a young *hazzan* to study with an established cantor and to marry into his family. While Max did not live with the Koerners, as might have his younger, European counterpart, he visited often with Koerner to study the older *hazzan*'s compositions and did, in fact, become engaged to his daughter Theresa, an accomplished pianist.

In the spring of 1934, the *Farband* recommended Max for a position in Cleveland. Unlike the usual "cattle-call" auditions where a number of applicants would be invited to come to a synagogue at the same time and wait their turn to be called to sing before a board or selection committee, the Cleveland audition was scheduled for Max alone. In later years, the Cantors Assembly of America would ensure that its members would not suffer the indignity of group auditions, but would be afforded an opportunity to lead a Shabbat service in the synagogue itself.

Max traveled to Cleveland, came before the committee, was questioned in a dignified manner, and replied in like fashion to the satisfaction of the group. He then sang selections from the Sabbath, High Holy Day, and festival liturgies as requested. Unlike many such auditions, Max's transportation to and from Cleveland was paid for by the congregation. All in all, he was satisfied with the reaction of the committee and felt, as he reported at home, that the job was "in the bag." He was not particularly surprised that he had not heard from the congregation by the end of the month because a number of candidates were being interviewed. But after several months had passed without word, Max tired of waiting and simply put the audition out of his mind. He then asked the *Farband* for another recommendation and was sent to Montreal to audition for Congregation Sha'arei Shamayim.

He arrived on a Friday afternoon and prepared himself for the Sabbath. He *davened* well on Friday evening and returned the next morning fresh and eager to continue. Upon entering the synagogue, he was asked by the rabbi if he were able to read the Torah and, if so, could he read the portion that very morning? With his usual chutzpah and delight in challenges, Max affirmed, "It will be no problem." In the Szatmar yeshiva, he had been accustomed to review the entire weekly portion in the customary manner: *shnayim mikroh v'ehod targum* (twice the reading and once the translation). He knew texts, and chanting the Torah held no mysteries for him, but willingness to chant a long portion without any preparation was foolhardy.

"After you've finished *Shaharit,* please continue with the Torah reading," he was told. He barely had time to glance at the *parasha* (portion) for that week, realizing with a start that it was a double portion, *tazriah-m'tzorah*, twice the usual length. Undaunted, he led services and during the Torah reading chanted with fluency and confidence. Knowing that he had done well, he returned to New York to await the congregation's answer. He was surprised not to hear from them. The High Holy Days came and went without a word from Canada. Later that year, and quite by chance, Max found out what had happened:

> At a meeting of the *Farband,* I overheard the placement chairman complaining in his usual autocratic way about difficult congregations, the problems they presented, and his own formula for disciplining them: "And so they asked for Wohlberg," he related. "They had their nerve, waiting until only two weeks before Rosh Hashanah." "What is that you're saying?" I asked. "Who asked for me?" "They did," Cantor Singer said. "The Montreal *shul* you tried out for." "But—I never heard about it," I protested. "Of course not! They waited too long—*I* told them no! They learned their lesson. Next time, they'll have to get back to me faster."[18]

A few months before the High Holy Days, the Cleveland congregation for which Max had auditioned telephoned him. The committee had voted to retain Max. But Theresa, Max's bride-to-be, wanted to remain near her family and was not looking forward to living in the Midwest, so Max declined the offer. An unexpected and ironic twist to this episode was that the *hazzan* finally hired in Cleveland was the selfsame Malek of Homonna, whom the young Max had followed around with paper and pencil in 1921. Malek, who had had no time to teach the youngster to read music, had become Max's substitute.

In 1935, Max and Theresa were married, and Max looked for a new position that was closer to home. He applied to the Inwood Hebrew Congregation, located on Vermilyea Avenue and 207th Street in the Inwood section of Manhattan. Max passed the preliminary hurdles and was invited for a final interview.

It was raining heavily, and upon entering the building, Max found himself confronted by a well-known agent, a Mr. Malloy (Jewish, despite his Irish-sounding name), who specialized in placing *hazzanim*. Malloy had brought a young man who was to try out that same evening. Also with them was the applicant's father.

Although it was then common for cantors to employ the services of an agent when looking for a position, Malloy knew Max as one who had consistently declined to use his services. Max aligned himself with some others who thought that using a *probbeh*-agent (audition agent) was undignified. The process of selection was also one in which they often found themselves as helpless pawns. Slobin describes the scene:

> [Some synagogues] . . . start competitive hearings right after Passover. . . . They stage preliminary hearings during the week . . . to determine who shall be the lucky winner for the coming Saturday. As the time toward the New Year approaches, the congregation resolves to divide one Saturday service among as many as four or five applicants.[19]

Meeting Malloy was distasteful to Max, who had always tried to avoid him. But here, they found themselves face-to-face. Trying to make light of the situation, Wohlberg quipped, "I see you're here with a candidate and his father while all I have is a wet umbrella." The quip went unappreciated. With what passed for amenities behind them, the four were seated in the back of the synagogue facing a small committee seated on the *bimah*. Malloy's candidate was asked to sing first. He had a very powerful baritone voice and sang "Uv'nuho Yomar" (When the Ark rested). Then Max was asked to come forward. Knowing that he could not top the other candidate vocally, he devised a plan to impress the committee as he walked toward the front of the sanctuary.

> "What will you sing?" he was asked. "Anything that you want," Max replied, confident as always. "You pick a text for me." "Perhaps you could sing "Tikanto Shabbos" [You instituted the Sabbath] for us?" someone queried. "Of course," Max answered. When offered a siddur, Max declined with a casual, offhand gesture. "I am acquainted with the text," he said, and proceeded to improvise on the spot, embellishing his recitative in the traditional manner and style that he had mastered.[20]

When Max returned to his seat, Malloy commented, "You have the job!" Max demurred and sat down, only to be summoned a short while later to a room in another part of the synagogue. The rabbi extended his hand, introduced the president, and began to discuss details of the position that they said had been awarded to Max. His *chutzpah* had carried the day again. He was the new cantor in Inwood.

For me and for many others, there was an admirable quality in the preferred anonymity of the donor whose contribution was announced ohn a nomen. *Intimately related to humility, anonymity was a virtue highly esteemed by our ancestors. There are times when self-assertion is to be encouraged.* Horav shemochal al k'vodo ein k'vodo mochul *["If a rabbi renounces his honor, it is not renounced," i.e., undue modesty may not be the best recourse] is a sound principle (B.* Kedushin *32;* Mishneh Torah, Talmud Torah *5:11). Surely the lot of musicologists and bibliographers would be better served if every author and composer would sign and date his creation. Publishers and arrangers are equally guilty in this respect. Note Jacob Sandler, unacknowledged composer of "Eili, Eili," Goldfarb and "Shalom Aleichem," "Kadesheinu," simultaneously attributed to Binder, Idelsohn, and Goldfarb.*

—Wohlberg, Pirkei Hazzanut, <i>The Cantors Voice</i> 5, no. 3
(April 1953)

5
ON TO INWOOD (1935–41)

In 1935, the Wohlbergs moved to upper Manhattan, where Max was to serve the Inwood Hebrew Congregation. Marvin S. Wiener (1925–), a young student in the Talmud Torah who would later become a rabbi and one of the first directors of the Cantors Institute, recalls with considerable affection his years as a member of Max's new congregation. Years later, Wiener would be in a position to recommend Max for a position in Malverne, Long Island.

Now able to concentrate fully on his cantorial duties, Max turned his considerable personal charm to the task of organizing an amateur congregational chorus. He was successful in bringing together thirty-five singers, and he learned to conduct through experience. Unlike the service-oriented choir that provided musical assistance only at religious services, this congregational group performed on other occasions. They sang arrangements of songs in Hebrew, Yiddish, and English.

Max's activity in this area was mirrored by other *hazzanim* and choral directors. Jews were beginning to look to the synagogue for activities more reflective of life in the secular community. The synagogue was losing its image as "an ethnicity based upon town of origin." As early as 1914, Mordecai Menahem Kaplan (1881–1983) had articulated the need for a new type of synagogue as part of his notion of Judaism as a "civilization." By the late 1910s, Jewish Americans had begun to gather in socio-musical groups. The leftist Workmen's Circle Chorus, the *Farband* Choral Society, the Cantors Chorus, and others not only satisfied musical longings but provided a forum for socializing (or, as in the case of the Workmen's Circle Chorus, a platform for championing a specific cause). As a logical outgrowth of this philosophy, the *hazzan* could look forward to increased demands on his musical skills.

Kaplan was born in the Russian Pale but was the product of an American education; he had even taken courses at the Seminary when he was twelve years old. While serving as rabbi of Orthodox Kehillat Jeshurun synagogue in New York, he became conflicted between his duties and presence as the rabbi of that synagogue versus his personal distancing from the traditional point of view (i.e., the immutability of Torah and the concept of the "chosen people") and his emerging philosophy of Judaism as a civilization. Contemplating leaving the rabbinate, Kaplan received Schechter's invitation to become dean of the Teachers Institute, thus "saving" him for the Seminary.

The ideas of Kaplan always provoked controversy among the Seminary faculty. The attack made on his "new" prayer book was well publicized, and his writings and lectures created understandable strain. Convinced that industrial and scientific advances canceled traditional pathways, he thought that Judaism should seek new and revolutionary byways in order to survive. He proved to be a major influence at the Seminary, the Teachers Institute, and in the United Synagogue of America.

Kaplan's linkage of synagogue and center was widely accepted, and Wohlberg, like many other *hazzanim* answering the community's call for addressing social and cultural issues under the umbrella of the synagogue-cum-center, complied. Wohlberg secured sheet music, a piano, and an accompanist, and organized and conducted a communal chorus that met in the synagogue building. This chorus performed for the membership of the synagogue, gave concerts in the community, and often performed with other choral groups. However, they did not sing on the Sabbath, at which time Wohlberg often conducted a professional quartet or octet of men and boys. In addition, he sang cantorial recitatives, solos with the choir, and duets (usually with a boy alto or a bass). Sabbath morning services were elaborate, continuing until 1:30 or 2:00 in the afternoon.

Congregations not only understood and appreciated such musical exposition, but felt cheated when services ended before early afternoon. Levine, commenting on practices at Chizuk Amuno Congregation in Baltimore, explains:

> Lean and unadorned prayer chant . . . essential during weekday services . . . was not true of Sabbath and festival mornings. On those occasions, most worshipers arrived in family groups after having eaten a light breakfast, which did not fall under the category of a "meal." Most important, they did not have to rush off to work afterward. The services, which lasted three hours, progressed at a more relaxed pace.[21]

On the High Holy Days, Max was accompanied by a professional choir of men, augmented with boy soloists. They were conducted by the composer Jacob Dymont (1881–1956), who arranged much of the music. Conducting choirs for the High Holy Days was the expected role for Jewish musicians capable of the task, and some, such as Dymont, supplemented their regular income in this manner. Others were full-time impresario-conductors, such as Meir Machtenberg (1885–1926) and Oscar Julius (1903–86), who trained a number of symphonic choirs and engaged other men to lead them. Many of these groups also sang at resort hotels during the Passover season. Among others who conducted choirs in this manner were Abraham Ellstein (1907–63), Zavel Zilberts (1881–1949), and Joseph Rumshinsky (1881–1956).

Max also taught in the congregational religious school, as he had done in College Point. He continued to study general and Jewish music and honed his skills as a *hazzan*. In spite of the traditional rivalry between rabbi and cantor—the uneasy working relationship between them probably developed after the arrival of European-ordained rabbis in the 1840s, who supplanted the earlier *hazzan*-ministers—Max consistently enjoyed good relationships with rabbis. His easygoing personality and delightful sense of humor stood him in good stead throughout his life.

Max studied other religions and Reform Judaism as well, often attending Rabbi Stephen Wise's Sunday morning services at Carnegie Hall. But Max felt most at home in the Conservative movement, and later became one of its champions.

It is of interest that, although the Seminary had first been organized in an effort to halt the spread of the Reform movement in America, Solomon Schechter assumed a conciliatory attitude toward the Reform, making friends with scholars in the movement, particularly with Kaufman Kohler (1843–1926). Kohler convened the Pittsburgh Conference of Reform Rabbis in 1885 and saw to the adoption of the so-called Pittsburgh Platform, which marked the beginning of the Reform movement in America. Kohler became president of Hebrew Union College in 1903. Schechter's policy was to avoid public condemnation of the Reform movement's policies and to remain on good terms with its leaders. His hope was to influence its direction through careful and patient dialogue.

Many of Wohlberg's contemporaries were part of what Schechter described as the new arrivals who brought with them their own experiences and rituals from Europe and who were seeking answers to religious and social problems. Stephen Wise, whose appearance and personal charisma matched his oratorical dynamism, was a very popular public lecturer at the time. Max, along with many others, was searching for theological answers, and was drawn to Wise's spellbinding performances that extolled the virtues of Reform Judaism. While always open to new thoughts and ideas, Max was intellectually uncomfortable with Reformist theology and rejected it as he had rejected Orthodoxy.

Leadership of congregations often changes rapidly, bringing to office successive presidents with divergent points of view, and the Inwood congregation was no exception. Of its internal politics at that time, Max later reminisced: "*Gei shlofn mit ein president und shtei oif mit a zweiten* [I would go to sleep with one president and wake up with another]."[22]

Because the congregation expected and encouraged his singing of long recitatives, Max was further compelled to expand his repertoire. He researched all available materials and, in the process, established guidelines for himself that became the norm for the *nusah hatefillah* in a future school for *hazzanim*, the Cantors Institute of the Jewish Theological Seminary of America. He described his search for music that was traditional and cleansed of artificial accretion:

> At the end of the twenties I began, and through the thirties I continued, a thorough study of literally every volume of synagogue music and every article dealing with Jewish music. From these I learned of national, regional, and local variations as well as of individual deviations in the subject of *nusah*.[23]

Many of the composers of the recitatives he selected were champions of the Eastern European style. These included Solomon Weintraub (1781–1829), Baruch Schorr (1823–1904), Baruch Leib Rozowski (1841–1919), Eliezer

Gerowitch (1844–1913), Pinchas Minkowski (1859–1924), Abraham Baer Birnbaum (1864–1922), and Abraham Moshe Bernstein (1866–1932).

As Max's reputation as a *hazzan* grew, so did attendance at services. There were always many visitors at services during Sabbaths and festivals, including a number of retired rabbis and cantors. Max recalled that one retired singer "with a tremendous voice" was known locally as the "Jewish Caruso." Friends of this man insisted that Max invite him to sing on a Sabbath morning: "It would be nice if you asked him to *daven far a shabbes.*" "Of course," was the easygoing reply, and arrangements were made for the man to lead services. Difficult and unpleasant, he arrived on the chosen day and bellowed his way through the prayers without art or subtlety, in contrast to the delicacy and good taste of Max's renditions. "Caruso's" supporters were shamed into silence.

Max sought new ways to involve worshipers in the service and began to write congregational tunes that were based upon *nusah hatefillah.* His lifelong pursuit would be to fill a musical void left by the loss of traditional *daveners* (congregational chanters). The Eastern European synagogue had been filled with what was described by Nehemia Mendelson as the sound of a "murmurai."

> The traditional Conservative service, with its core of what today's *hazzanim* call "real *daveners,*" was in many ways participatory, with the *hazzan* displaying his leadership largely through recitatives, fantasia-like breaks in the communal action, to highlight a certain text. What few tunes there were would be rhythmic or lyrical relief phrases, offering welcome contrast to the roulades and flourishes of an intricate recitative or choir piece.[24]

Wohlberg turned his melodic gift to the task of creating tunes that he called "congregational-oriented and that could be sung *bin'imah*—pleasingly." These early efforts later surfaced in the publication of his first book of congregational songs, *Shirei Zimrah.*[25] Max wrote comprehensively on the subject and stressed the Conservative origin of a practice that had become widespread:

> It was in the Conservative synagogue in the United States that congregational singing of the liturgy in Hebrew achieved its greatest popularity. There, as in no other place, it was welcomed and there it flourished. It has since been adopted in Orthodox and Reform congregations.[26]

Max spent countless hours in the major libraries of New York City reading books and articles on Jewish music, continuing his regimen of self-study. He became known as a writer and lecturer in the greater New York community, contributing articles to the Yiddish newspapers, lecturing on Jewish music to university students, and speaking on radio station WQXR.

Through the *Farband,* Max established a close relationship with David Roitman, Zavel Kwartin, and other *hazzanim.* He became particularly friendly with Kwartin, their relationship dating back to Max's childhood, when he had heard Kwartin sing in Budapest. Although Kwartin had a marvelous voice and unique style, his formal training in music was minimal. Max visited him often in Brooklyn, and on one such visit, Kwartin sat at the piano in his living room and asked Max to sing.

> "I'll accompany you," he said. "What shall I sing?" asked Max. "Ato Nigleiso" [You revealed Yourself] was Kwartin's suggestion. "Sing, Wohlberg, I'll play. The best key for a *hazzan* to sing in is the key of F." Kwartin played four unison Fs on the piano. Max began to sing, warming to the task, improvising and leaving the key of F far behind as he modulated, while Kwartin, totally unperturbed, continued to sound the same four Fs.[27]

Through his friends, Max became involved in the inner workings of the *Hazzanim Farband,* first as a member of the board of directors and then as recording secretary in Yiddish. It was well known that the *Farband* was a friendly place to spend time but had very little clout in the real business of cantorial placement. The building on Second Avenue and Houston Street was called the *kibbetzarnyeh* (hangout), a place to come to *shmooz* (casual conversation), to play a game of cards, and to hold impromptu vocal contests.[28]

Until the relatively recent establishment of the modern cantorial bodies, cantorial placement was a serious problem. In 1940, it was determined that only 20 percent of all *hazzanim* had annual positions. Slobin quotes Joshua Weisser:

> Those chosen for the few existing jobs are cantorially illiterate . . . selected on the basis of a few *shtickelech* [tricks] they picked up from listening to phonograph records. . . . The genuine *hazzan* who spent most of his life studying . . . is overlooked.[29]

This situation was exacerbated by the struggle for jobs between recent refugees and those already in place in America, as another commentator recorded: "The young ones have the advantage, first because you have to read certain prayers in English, which is a bit stiff for the older *hazzanim,* and second, because you have to please the ladies."[30]

This state of affairs was the inevitable result of certain practices initiated by New York congregations that, as far back as 1885, competed with one another for "star" *hazzanim,* leading to a cantorial migration to America in 1885–86, where each new arrival was filled with the hope that he would gather up "fistfuls of gold" in the New World. Congregations soon decided not to wait and see who stepped off the boat but to take the initiative, and they began to import European *hazzanim,* many from Lithuania. The president of the *Farband* admitted that the association had failed to find jobs for most of its members. A heated series of debates followed on whether the *Farband* should link arms with organized labor in order to force congregations to adopt policies favorable to legitimate *hazzanim.* Max voiced his opposition with conviction: "Lay leaders [do not] make a living from my singing. What will the union threaten them with? We are clergymen. What do we have to do with a labor union?"[31] He later recounted that one outspoken protagonist for a merger with the American Federation of Labor exhorted heatedly: "We'll fight them [congregations, managers, etc.] in the streets. *Blut vet sich giessen* [blood will flow]!"[32]

Only two members spoke out against the motion to join the union: Leib Glantz and Wohlberg. When the ballots were tallied, only one vote had been cast against the move; Glantz had abstained. Indeed, the membership did vote overwhelmingly to join hands with the union, and on August 21, 1942, they became the Cantors Ministers Union No. 20804, chartered by the AF of L. The association was short-lived. The union members refused to picket synagogues, and the *Farband* membership refused to pay dues. Their dissolution was by mutual agreement!

During these tumultuous days in the early history of the *Farband,* Max longed for the scholarly give and take that would characterize his later correspondence. In an effort to provide a cultural forum for *hazzanim,* in 1938 he joined with Leib Glantz and Adolph Katchko in organizing the Cantors Ministers Cultural Organization (also known as the *Chazzanim Ministers Alliance-K'neset Hachazzanim D'New York*). This group lasted only a short time but served as a bridge from the *Farband* to the organizations of the post–World War II period.

Their agenda, meetings, discussions, priorities, grievances, petulancies, and peeves may well be unique to this period in the history of American *hazzanut*. An accurate accounting of those meetings and a wonderful cameo of the personalities that went with the voices is faithfully and impartially recorded by Wohlberg, while he served as the recording secretary. In an article written for the Cantors Assembly publication, *Journal of Synagogue Music,* Wohlberg asks for a future history of the cantorate and offers the minutes as the "early efforts of a few cantors who wished to refashion the character of the cantorate in America and to divert its course into new channels."[33]

The accounts were derived from his own handwritten notes, which cover the period of December 7, 1938, to January 31, 1940. The pithy notes bespeak volumes when read in context and paint a picture of a cantorate in search of itself. (Rather than offering a summation here, the writer refers the reader to appendix D of this volume.)

In 1941, Theresa gave birth to a son, Jeffrey, who is now a rabbi. The *b'rit millah* (circumcision) was a happy affair where Max's famous friends Zavel Kwartin and David Roitman were in attendance, and Roitman sang in honor of the occasion. Faced with the need for a better salary because of his growing family, Max thought that now might be a good time to look for a different position, and he applied to Beth El Congregation in Minneapolis. After meeting with a small committee in New York, Max was invited to travel to Minneapolis for a weekend to lead services and meet the congregants. The trip proved successful, and Max was appointed the new *hazzan* of Beth El.

Risking the rabbinic dictum S'tam makshon am ho'oretz *["At the risk of appearing foolish"], I nonetheless wish to pose some questions whose answers elude me. One of the quips in* yeshivot *of old was* Freg mir a kashe, ich hob a teretz *["Ask me a question (because) I have an answer"]. However, let me assure you that I have no satisfactory solutions. (1) How can one replace an old tune cherished by the congregation without raising the ire of our congregants? (2) Since great portions of our liturgy have been eliminated from the service, how can we save their tunes? (3) How can we express in song the loss that our generation witnessed, that of the Holocaust? (4) How can we reflect the rebirth of Israel, its pulse, rhythm, accents, and flavor, in our worship?*

—Wohlberg, Pirkei Hazzanut, *The Cantors Voice* 11, no. 2 (May 1961)

6
NORTHWARD BOUND: MINNEAPOLIS (1941–45)

Max took an instant liking to Minneapolis and to Beth El, which had a fine amateur chorus that included many students from the local colleges. He led the choir on Shabbat, and a conductor was engaged for the High Holy Days. Unlike College Point and Inwood, Max was not required to teach in the religious school because Beth El's children attended a Talmud Torah, thus freeing Max to devote himself completely to music.

During his first year at Beth El, Max took a fourteen-year-old boy under his wing and taught him how to chant all the prayers for the High Holy Days so that the boy could lead the synagogue's auxiliary service. They studied together from March through August, two hours a day, five days a week. The experience changed the life of the youngster, Morton Leifman (1926–), who became a rabbi as well as dean of the Cantors Institute and the College of Jewish Music of the Jewish Theological Seminary of America with Max as the head of its department of *nusah*. Of that time with Max in Minneapolis, Leifman commented: "I found that I could express my religious emotions in singing the liturgy. . . . I was launched. My interest in things Jewish began to flower with music as the core."[34]

Beth El's service contrasted markedly with those of Ahavas Achim and the Inwood Hebrew Congregation. Max had created many traditional-style recitatives for his own use in his former congregations. At Beth El, he found a service more congenial to choral and congregational song rather than to cantorial solo. As is often the case, service requirements and musical forces available to a composer of synagogue music determine the direction of his creativity. The choral forces at Beth El provided Max with an opportunity to develop his compositional technique in writing for a choir. His first pieces for mixed chorus appeared at this time.

In Rabbi David Aronson (1894–1988), Max found a sympathetic and considerate coworker, and their relationship was marked by mutual respect. A scholar, Aronson was curious about his new *hazzan;* cantorial ability and knowledge of Judaica did not always go hand in hand. Already impressed with Max's cantorial skills and wanting to question him on his knowledge of Judaica, Aronson took from his shelf a book containing laws, blessings, and customs written in Seville in 1340 by David Ben Joseph Abudarham. Max glanced at an open page, immediately recognizing it. "Oh, how very nice!" he exclaimed. "I see you have an Abudarham." The questioning session was over before it had begun.

At Beth El, it was customary to have a party at the conclusion of Simhat Torah, and Max was asked to prepare a program for the occasion. He rewrote the words to the well-known Yiddish song "A Chazzandl af Shabbes" (the story of a hazzan who comes to a congregation in search of a position). Max's version told of three congregants who went to find a hazzan. They were Rabbi and Mrs. Aronson and Beth El's president. In Max's rendition, each of the three looked for something different: "The rabbi wanted a yodeia seifer [scholar], the rebbetzin (rabbi's wife) was interested in a man who made a nice appearance, while the president sought a hazzan who could sing a good Hashkiveinu [evening prayer for peace]."[35] The congregation was delighted to have found a cantor who was not only creative but had a good sense of humor.

At this time, Max was invited to contribute articles on Jewish music to the *Universal Jewish Encyclopedia.* Beginning with volume 3, he was listed as a contributing editor. He wrote cantorial biographies and monographs on Jewish music in general.

Max had been a reasonably good soccer player in his youth in Europe, and in Minneapolis he discovered that he had a penchant for handball. Small in stature and with quick reflexes, Max became a familiar sight on the courts. He entered handball competitions, and in 1943–44 teamed up with a partner who was 6 foot 5. The diminutive Max and his towering companion were often referred to as David and Goliath and achieved moderate success in four-wall handball, winning match after match in the national championships of 1944, until they reached the semifinals.

Meanwhile, marital difficulties had surfaced, causing much tension in the Wohlberg household. Although Max felt that he had found the congregation and the city where he could spend the rest of his career, Theresa hated Minneapolis from the beginning and wanted desperately to return to the East. In an effort to keep his small family intact, Max unhappily decided to leave the congregation in which he had found such satisfaction. He began to search for a congregation near New York City and learned from the *Farband* of a cantorial vacancy in Hartford, Connecticut. After applying to Emanu El there, he met with its rabbi, Morris Silverman, and a committee, and was hired. In July 1945, Max, Theresa, and Jeffrey moved to Hartford for what would be a one-year stay.

Although most historians are of the opinion that the hero is the creation of his era rather than its creator, the validity of this opinion is still a fair topic for discussion. While on one side we may argue that the source of ideas and the materials employed by the innovator may, as a rule, be traced to the theories and works of his predecessors, on the other side we know of men in diverse fields who are "ahead of their generation," whose ideas are not accepted by their contemporaries. Regrettably, the sources out of which the "history of hazzanut" *could be fashioned lie untapped, and the materials for its building remain scattered in unsuspected places.*

—Wohlberg, Pirkei Hazzanut, *The Cantors Voice* 6, no. 3 (May 1954)

7
A BRIEF VISIT: HARTFORD (1945–46)

At first sight, Emanu El was impressive. The substantial and lofty building was a landmark in Hartford, and the congregation enjoyed a good reputation as a leader in the community. The rabbi was the scholarly Morris Silverman, who wrote a manuscript that would become the basis of the *Sabbath and Festival Prayer Book,* which was published in 1946 by the Rabbinical Assembly of America and the United Synagogue of America. A large professional choir and organ were available to assist the *hazzan.* Although Theresa seemed placated by the move to Hartford, Max was dissatisfied with the position from the onset. It was one of the few occasions in his professional life when he was not empathetic with the congregation and its rabbi. While Max would later counsel his students not to be in a hurry to change positions but to give themselves time to adjust to the congregation, their tasks, and the other professionals, no sooner had he arrived at Emanu El than he began looking for an opportunity to leave.

Max again turned to the *Farband* for placement and was informed that Rabbi Leon Lang of Philadelphia, the son-in-law of *hazzan*-composer Sholom Greenspan (also known as Sholom Ananiever [1857–??]), was looking for a *hazzan.* Max took a train to Philadelphia and upon his arrival was upset to see that other *hazzanim* were waiting for their turn to sing, and Max was at the end of the line. He had arrived at a cantorial "cattle call," about which the *Farband* had not warned him. It was late when the other candidates had finished singing, and Max was tired after the long train ride. No questions were asked of any candidate. Loudness of singing seemed to be the only requirement.

Finally, Max was called forward and asked to perform but he wanted to talk about the position and his qualifications for it before he sang. There was a short discussion, and the chairman responded, "We're only interested in how you sing." "You see," returned Max easily, "why should I sing if we know in advance that the job is not for me?" He shook hands politely and left the synagogue, returning to Hartford that night.

During 1945–46, Max met several times with Rabbi Max Arzt (1897–1975) at the Jewish Theological Seminary to explore the possibility of the Seminary's establishing a school for the training of American *hazzanim*. During the Holocaust, the wellsprings of traditional *hazzanut*, which were the Jewish communities of the Old World, had been demolished. In order for the cantorate to continue in America, it was necessary to establish cantorial schools to replace the apprentice system of Europe. In one of their meetings, Arzt told Max that Rabbi Lang had left his congregation and was now rabbi of Beth El in West Philadelphia. He was looking for a *hazzan*, but this time for his new congregation. Max applied to Beth El, took an instant liking to Rabbi Lang and the congregation, and was hired on the spot.

That Wohlberg's meetings with Max Arzt regarding the Seminary's housing a school for *hazzanim* were not premature but rather overdue is evidenced by the early activities of the Jewish Ministers Cantors' Association. Aware of the need for such a school, they had, in the 1920s, undertaken through concerts (1920, -21, -24, -26, and -27) in Madison Square Garden, Carnegie Hall, Mecca Temple, and Rodeph Shalom in New York to raise funds that would be used to open a cantorial school. The large sums of money raised were eventually used for purposes other than the creation of a cantorial seminary, but the concerts were tangible signs that the idea of such an educational institution had been floating around for years.

The Wohlberg/Arzt meetings may have been precipitated by an exceptional meeting in 1944 in Atlantic City by a group of *hazzanim* who gathered to plan for a national cantors' school. The idea was to form an institution where Orthodox, Reform, and Conservative students might learn the cantorial craft together. As recalled by former Philadelphia lawyer/*hazzan* W. Belskin Ginsberg (1898–1982), the idea was enthusiastically received but failed to receive support, particularly from the New York contingent. As Leeser's Maimonides College (1867–73) had opened and soon closed primarily because of lack of financial support from New York rabbis, so this idea of a cantorial seminary never made it off the drawing board for want of support from New York *hazzanim*. By good fortune, the Seminary itself had found its financial champion in Cyrus Adler and had survived and flourished; and it was the Seminary that would provide a home for the future cantorial school.

This happened through the persuasive efforts of a brand-new body, the Cantors Assembly of America, which was organized mainly by David Putterman (1900–1979) with the assistance of Wohlberg, Ginsberg, and others. The Cantors Assembly, now the world's largest professional organization for *hazzanim*, was created in Putterman's home in New York in 1947. Putterman, the longtime *hazzan* of Park Avenue Synagogue in New York as well as the director of the department of music of the United Synagogue, became the Assembly's first executive director. The Assembly's primary objective was to create a school for cantors housed in the Seminary.

The concept for a traditional cantorial school moved forward, particularly when a Reform rival, the School of Sacred Music, opened successfully in New York in 1948. Hebrew Union College in Cincinnati had sent Abraham Franzblau (1901–82)—assisted by Jewish music historian and activist Eric Werner (1901–88)—to its sister school on Sixty-Eighth Street in New York to establish a school of education as well as what was to be a nondenominational school for cantors. Envisioned was a program that trained cantors for Orthodox, Conservative, and Reform congregations. The School of Sacred Music became a reality, and its faculty consisted of well-known cantorial teachers from the Orthodox as well as the Reform movement. A board of certification was also established, which examined cantors already in the field who had not undergone formalized training and awarded them certification on merit. The school offered a course of study that led to certification as cantor-educator (and, in rare instances, that of cantor alone). Hebrew Union College merged with the Jewish Institute of Religion in 1950 and became known as HUC-JIR. In June 1954, the School of Sacred Music inaugurated a four-year program leading to the Bachelor of Sacred Music degree. Recently reorganized as a graduate institution, the school now requires that incoming students already have a Bachelor of Music degree.[36]

In 1948, at the first annual convention of the Cantors Assembly, a spirited discussion about the creation of a Conservative cantorial school took place, with speeches by Seminary chancellor Louis Finkelstein (1895–1991), Simon Greenberg (1901–1991), Albert Gordon (1903–68), and others. There was a sense of urgency to begin the project.

While still in Minneapolis, Max had also discussed with fellow Minneapolis resident Rabbi Albert Gordon (1903–68) ways in which the Seminary might be home to such a school. In 1949, Gordon assumed duties in New York as executive director of the United Synagogue. There he and Rabbi Moshe Davis (1919–96) joined forces with Max and David Putterman to persuade Chancellor Louis Finkelstein to offer a summer cantorial course at the Seminary as an experiment.

Fourteen *hazzanim* gathered at the Seminary in July 1950 for classes led by composer and anthologist Chemjo Vinaver (1900–1974), composer Mark Silver (1892–1963), rabbinic scholar Moshe Zucker (1902–87), and Wohlberg. Delighted with the results, Putterman and Wohlberg joined with representatives of the Seminary in establishing the Seminary College of Jewish Music and the Cantors Institute of the Jewish Theological Seminary. These became the first schools of Jewish music in America authorized to grant academic degrees, and were formally inaugurated on September 14, 1952. The Seminary presented a certificate of appreciation to the Cantors Assembly of America in recognition of the Assembly's efforts on its behalf. The College of Jewish Music would grant the academic degrees of Master of Sacred Music as well as doctorates in the field; the Cantors Institute would grant certification as "*hazzan* in Israel."

―――――〰―――――

Vienna, like no other city, for over a hundred years served as the place where hazzanut *of every type and shade was represented. The influence of Solomon Sulzer reached beyond the walls of the Seitenstettengasse Temple. The cantors Adolph Fischer and Isak Schiller valiantly tried to emulate the great master. His ultimate successor, Josef Singer, and the great virtuoso Josef Goldstein introduced the Hungarian tradition, with its strict adherence to the minutiae of* nusah. *The Turkish synagogue and its influential cantor, Jacob Bauer, added a new Sephardic ingredient. Great vocalists like Bela Guttman and Don Fuchs (who succeeded Goldstein and Singer, respectively) contributed luster to the multicolored cantorial symphony. The Eastern European style was introduced at first by itinerant* hazzanim, *then by men like Mayer Schorr, Pesach Feinsinger, Josef Morgenstern, Boruch Frankel, Leibush Miller, Gershon Margolies, and Samuel Postulow. Add to these a number of Hassidic rebbes who made Vienna their headquarters, and you have a perfect opportunity for fusion and amalgam.*

—Wohlberg, Pirkei Hazzanut, *The Cantors Voice* 9, no. 1 (November 1957)

―――――〰―――――

8
PHILADELPHIA: FIRST ENCOUNTER (1946–57)

The largest city in Pennsylvania and one of the principal cities of the northeastern United States, Philadelphia is known for its important role in U.S. history. Jews were active in business in colonial Philadelphia as early as the mid-eighteenth century. High Holy Day services were held there in 1761 with a "scroll of the Law" borrowed from Congregation Shearith Israel in New York "in order to fulfill the biblical injunction."[37] By 1830 and the arrival of Isaac Leeser, "who emerged as the leading Jew not only of the city but the whole country," the Philadelphia community had been in existence for almost a century.[38] Although relatively small in number, the Jewish community in Philadelphia was an important one and established patterns of survival and growth that successive generations of Jewish immigrants followed in other cities.[39] When the Wohlbergs arrived in 1946, the Jewish community in Philadelphia was well on its way to becoming one of the largest enclaves of Conservative Judaism in the world.

At Beth El, Max found a fine professional quartet and organist and a service that was dignified and inspiring. A well-subsidized congregation, the synagogue had been built by a Philadelphia member of the Rothschild family as a memorial to his first wife. A Conservative congregation, Beth El still used the so-called Jastrow prayer book, a more traditional effort than the Reform prayer book that had been widely used by many congregations. The former *hazzan* of the congregation, an elderly man named Winokur, had served the synagogue for twenty-seven years. After Max's arrival, Winokur attended services regularly, sitting directly in front of Max in the first row. As Max sang, Winokur would sound his tuning fork, checking Max's high notes.

Max had become impatient with casual attitudes toward *nusah hatefillah* and decided to embark on a major "clean-up" campaign in his new synagogue. The process was not uneventful. Max changed the music of the congregational responses in the *Shaharit Kedushah* (morning sanctification) from a major key to the synagogue mode *Ahava Rabba* ("with great love"; a major third and a minor second give this mode a Middle Eastern flavor). According to traditional practice, responses at this point in the service should be in the same musical mode as the *Ahava Rabba* of the cantorial passages. At Beth El, they were not; Beth El congregants had long been accustomed to singing the responses in major (without the minor second). Not consulting anyone, Max rewrote the congregational responses in the proper mode, *Ahava Rabba*.

On the following Sabbath, the congregation tried to follow the choir in the new arrangement. It didn't work out: the congregation stopped, started, and stopped again, completely confused. After services, the rabbi and the president confronted Max, who explained the musical differences. The president replied, "It's interesting, '*hazzen*' [Yiddish colloquial], but to tell you the truth, I couldn't care less!" Unfazed, Max returned to the old responses but inserted the new melody he had written in *Ahava Rabba* into other places in the service. He and the choir sang many texts to that same tune for the next four weeks. The congregation heard that melody from the moment they walked into the synagogue until the final amen. On the fifth week, the tune was not heard until the service reached the *Shaharit Kedushah*. There the congregants sang the response to the new *Ahava Rabba* melody with gusto, as though it were an old friend. Max had learned how to prepare congregants for musical changes. As he would advise his students later: "Make changes slowly and prepare your congregation for them."

While preparing for his first High Holy Days at Beth El, Max was confronted with a *piyyut* (liturgical poem) unknown to him. It had a prominent place in the *Ne'ilah* (closing of the heavenly gates to prayer) service at the end of Yom Kippur. The poem, "Eil Norah Alilah" (God revered and sublime), and its joyous tune are traditional to Sephardic Jews. In Philadelphia, the melody and poem were popular because of the influence of the Spanish-

Portuguese ritual as practiced at Philadelphia's Sephardic congregation, Mikveh Israel. But neither text nor tune was within the experience of the former student of the Szatmar yeshiva. It was natural, then, for Max to write his own melody and to sing it with the choir. A congregant approached him after *Ne'ilah*. "Why didn't you sing the right melody for 'Eil Norah'?" he asked. Max promised to restore the tune to its rightful place. This incident served to arouse his interest in Sephardic music, elements of which he later integrated into his own compositions.

Max was active in the Philadelphia branch of the Cantors Assembly and in 1948 was elected the national president of the Cantors Assembly of America, a position he held until 1951. He also became conductor of the Cantors' Choir of Philadelphia and in that capacity invited guests from New York to perform with the group. When Moshe Koussevitsky arrived for a concert with the choir, Max rearranged Zeidel Rovner's "Emet Ve'emuna" (True and faithful) for the occasion. Following the successful concert, Koussevitsky, a large and effusive man, wrapped the diminutive Max in a bear hug and almost carried him off the stage. The president of the Philadelphia region of the Assembly approached the two and greeted them with:

> "*Tsvei Moishes! A groiser Moishe un a kleiner Moishe* [Two Moshes! A big Moshe and a small Moshe]!" The irrepressible Koussevitsky rejoined gleefully without pause, "Why do you call me a *kleiner Moishe?*"[10]

Cantorial training in the United States prior to World War II was not that different from the European manner. But it was not the same, either. It would have been rare in America for a youngster to become a long-term apprentice to a practicing *hazzan*, living with him and learning his music. However, home, neighborhood, and religious training were still important factors, as they had been in Europe. Cantorial training in America was limited to the metropolitan areas where master teachers taught, supplied music, and were on the lookout for positions for some of their students. The tutorial system of cantorial teaching still prevailed; to study for the cantorate, one found a cantor who could teach. If the aspirant were lucky, a single teacher could supply appropriate music and teach it by rote if necessary. More often, one went from one cantor or choir director to another. In Slobin's *Chosen Voices,* Lawrence Avery (1927–) comments on his days as a student:

> [T]here were teachers . . . Lipitz there, Berman there, Raisin there, and Beimel here. . . . Katchko was another. . . . [H]e wrote me the entire repertoire, handwritten.[11]

In the early days of the Cantors Institute, Hugo Weisgall (1913–97), a well-known opera composer, was appointed faculty chairman. With great foresight, he and the first director of the school, Rabbi Max Routtenberg (1909–87), gathered together a formidable faculty: Joseph Yasser (1893–1981), a highly respected musicologist and organist; Near Eastern and Indian music specialist Johanna Spector (1915–), who established the Institute's department of ethnomusicology; Solomon Rosowsky (1878–1962), composer, one of the last remaining members of the Saint Petersburg Society for Jewish Folk Music (the seminal group of Russian-Jewish composers and musicologists who took to heart their teacher Rimsky-Korsakoff's admonition "find your own musical heritage and build upon it") and codifier of the Lithuanian-Palestinian tropal system; Siegfried Landau (1921–), composer and orchestral conductor; Albert Weisser (1920–84), author, composer, musicologist, and bibliophile; well-known *hazzanim* and formidable teachers of the cantorial art Moshe Taubé (1927–) and David Koussevitsky (1911–85); Rabbi Marvin Wiener, instructor in Judaica; and others from the Seminary faculty.

The student body was generally well versed in music and had accumulated years of experience as performers. Some among them had excellent Jewish backgrounds from yeshiva studies and from singing in the choirs of well-known *hazzanim*. Classes were, and continue to be, relatively small, affording much opportunity for individual work.

During 1951, before the official opening of the schools, Max traveled to New York from Philadelphia twice each week, teaching *nusah* and working on a curriculum for his courses. The teachers of *hazzanut,* both in Europe and in America, taught *nusah* based upon their own experience, which depended upon their country of origin and the material given them by their own teachers. Not only do Eastern and Western European traditions differ in many respects, but regional variations exist to a great extent. Max thought that such a one-sided approach was not correct; he wanted *hazzanim* to be exposed to all existing traditions. He formulated a curriculum based upon an analyses of Eastern, Western, and Central European *hazzanut,* which permitted the student to select a suitable personal style based upon full knowledge of all available material. Max chose the *Ba'al Tefillah* of Abraham Baer (1834–94) as the reference for his classes in *nusah*. This cantorial compendium covers the liturgical year and offers variant examples of the same texts. Max also included materials that he had heard from *hazzanim* in Czechoslovakia, Hungary, and Rumania. He explained:

> I had learned of national, regional, and local variations and individual deviations in *nusah*. Incorporated into the curriculum were the results of discussions on the "aspects of *nusah*," which I had with *hazzanim* and composers such as Kwartin, Katchko, Weisser, Beimel, Jassinowski, Binder, and Glantz. On the other hand, contrary to my own assessment, some fine exponents of *hazzanim* such as Hershman, Kapov-Kagan, and Shlisky considered what they learned as youngsters to be the only correct version of *nusah*.[12]

In a philosophy akin to the historical approach of Zacharias Frankel (1801–75), who had concluded that a response was necessary to a traditional Judaism that was a changing and developing entity, Max thought that Old World–style, word-repetitive, and very florid recitatives had little place in the modern service; but he was unwilling to discard an entire repertoire of solo pieces in the name of progress and modernity. Like Frankel and his German contemporaries, Max postulated that Jewish music could adjust to the spirit of the time but should be able, in some measure, to resist it. He wanted the traditional style to be studied and analyzed as authentic examples, but ones that might no longer be appropriate for many congregations:

> I decided to acquaint our students with the totality of *hazzanut* and to give them samples of the recitatives that they will hear recorded by the "star" *hazzanim* of a previous generation, recitatives that I would not normally recommend for general use.[13]

In this respect, Wohlberg was in consonance with the Seminary's Mordecai Kaplan, who, at the same time, was teaching that "while the study of Jewish tradition is motivated by the purpose of finding direction for the future . . . it fosters a feeling of continuity with the past without enslaving one to it."[14]

As a composer of cantorial recitative, Max Wohlberg is most accurately characterized as a melodist, sensitive to the interpretive nuances inherent in liturgical texts. His most distinctive musical contribution is in the area of the unaccompanied recitative. His later recitatives are noteworthy for their interpretive character, economy of means, bold and unexpected modulations, lines that are unforced and natural, and an adherence to his concept of *ne'imah* (beauty, melodiousness). In his solo recitatives, Wohlberg distilled an elaborate and much ornamented song form into one that was linear and restrained.

Wohlberg's compositions generally have an authenticity that is derived from the abundance of cantillation and synagogal motives that they incorporate. Phrases of Yiddish songs and characteristics of Israeli folk melodies also appear in his compositions—all acquired through his lifelong exposure to musical aspects of Jewish life and reinforced through his teaching and research. The musical quotations or variations on them are effortlessly integrated into the composition. As well, whether intentional or not, quotations of sacred motives connect the text with the music's original or historical source.

His general style reflects the romanticism of the late nineteenth century. He passionately pursued proper Hebrew accentuation and tried to avoid tonal tedium. Like synagogue composer Israel Alter and others who spoke Yiddish and were immersed in its rich literature, the poetic foot of dactyl (two unstressed syllables following a stressed syllable) subtly signaled for a musical meter marking of 3/8, 6/8, or 3/4, which almost became a Wohlberg trademark. "If the piece is written in triple time, think Wohlberg" was an oft-heard expression. For example: "*Sho*-lem a /*lei*-chem, Reb/*Al*-ter?" ("*How* do you/*do*, Mis-ter/*Al*-ter?").[45]

During his son Jeffrey's summer days at Camp Ramah, Max began his annual visits to what he termed the Conservative movement's "hot-houses for the future of Conservative Judaism in the United States." Many rabbis and congregational leaders had their first taste of traditional Judaism in the Ramah camps. It was through these visits and his informal instruction that the practice of chanting *V'ahavta* according to the biblical tropal signs and the adoption of his tunes for the *Shabbat Avot* became associated with Shabbat worship in the Conservative movement.

In 1956, Max and Theresa divorced. The following year, Max married a member of his congregation, Miriam Wachsler. Rabbi Marvin Wiener, a former youth in Max's Inwood congregation and now director of the Cantors Institute, knew that the Malverne Jewish Center on Long Island in New York was in need of a *hazzan* and that the trip from Philadelphia to New York was becoming difficult for Max. Wiener recommended Max for the position, and the match was made. Max moved to Malverne with Miriam and Jeffrey.

―――――∞―――――

It is, I daresay, a fallacy that only the most outstanding or most popular composer leaves his imprint on the artists of his age and exerts his influence on the progress of his art. Often the art of the genius is inimitable and individualistic beyond emulation. Frequently, upon analysis, when frill and tinsel are eliminated, the admired masterpiece loses all attraction. More often than not, it is the quiet and unassuming practitioner who, shunning the limelight and evading publicity, patiently and without fanfare plods steadfastly and creates works of manifest value and of enduring quality. The loud blast may be sounded, but it is the still, small voice that is heard.

Wohlberg, Pirkei Hazzanut, *The Cantors Voice* 10, no. 1 (February 1959)

―――――∞―――――

9
ON TO LONG ISLAND: MALVERNE (1958–72); LONG BEACH (1972–78)

Malverne nestles into the south shore of Long Island in Nassau County. After 1950, and coinciding with the Wohlbergs' move to Malverne, Long Island's population increased tremendously—between 1950 and 1960, Nassau County grew from 672,765 to 1,300,171. The flood of new residents came mostly from the crowded streets of Brooklyn and the Bronx, and the new Jewish population of Long Island established a large number of active congregations, such as the Malverne Jewish Center. Located on Norwood Avenue, the synagogue was a short walk from the gracious home on Ogston Terrace that had been purchased for the Wohlbergs by the congregation.

From 1958 to 1972, Max continued to spend much of his time teaching at the Cantors Institute while functioning as the congregational *hazzan* of the Malverne Jewish Center. He taught music in the religious school, organized and developed an amateur choir, and established a close relationship with the rabbi, Samuel Chiel. In 1967, the Seminary recognized Max's efforts on behalf of the Cantors Institute and the cause of Jewish music by awarding him an honorary doctorate.

While in Malverne, Max composed many of his best works, particularly his unaccompanied recitatives. He developed a unique and modern style that found immediate acceptance among the students of the Cantors Institute. In workshops and in the classroom, Max earned an enviable reputation for artistic improvisations that modulated from key to key. He eschewed the tonal boredom of a one-key relationship in long texts and developed an ability to modulate skillfully within the Jewish modes.

In keeping with his recently developed spare but textually reflective style, Max collaborated with this writer on a number of projects, among them a traditional weekday *Ma'ariv* (evening) service that captured the essential elements of the traditional *nusah hatefillah* in an economical but moving manner.

Miriam's eyesight was failing, and Max increasingly assumed responsibility for her daily care. He had relied greatly upon Miriam to type the many articles and essays that he wrote, and her loss of vision diminished his output in this area.

In 1972, Max retired from the active cantorate and devoted himself to research, composing, lecturing, and the Cantors Institute. He moved from Malverne to the nearby town of Long Beach, where he became a member of Congregation Beth Shalom. There, the *hazzan*, Solomon Mendelson (1933–   ), one of the first graduates of the Cantors Institute, and his wife, Emma, were close friends of Max's. Mendelson was the nephew of Nehemiah Mendelson, who had been the *hazzan* of the Montreal congregation where Max had auditioned and read Torah many years previously. Both Mendelsons served as president of the Cantors Assembly of America.

Although he had officially retired from the pulpit, Max was often called upon to substitute for other *hazzanim*. On one occasion, he was asked to substitute for the *hazzan* at the *Selihot* (midnight penitential) service in the Kew Garden Hills section of Queens. Max was called on a Thursday and received the music on Friday. He looked it over on Saturday afternoon and, with no time for even a run-through with the choir, led *Selihot* that night. The service went well despite the fact that, while Max was singing, the choir director passed him some solos, duets, and trios that he had forgotten to give him the day before. Unfazed, Max sight-read the music.

By this time, Miriam had suffered three heart attacks and had lost her sight. In 1978, the Wohlbergs moved to Philadelphia for the support that would be offered by Miriam's two sisters and their families.

The problem of music in the Conservative synagogue, stated simply, is this: while our worshipers are, in the main, influenced by music of the so-called Eastern European type, music of excessive length, inordinate vocalization, and repetitive recitatives are frowned upon. Music that conforms both to good, old-fashioned chazonus *and to modern form is not abundantly available.*

—Wohlberg, Pirkei Hazzanut, *The Cantors Voice* 2, no. 6 (June 1951)

10
PHILADELPHIA: SECOND TIME AROUND (1978–94)

The Wohlbergs settled into an apartment on Tremont Street in northeast Philadelphia. Miriam suffered a final heart attack and died in 1980. She was buried in Roosevelt Cemetery in Philadelphia.

Max continued to travel to New York to teach at the Cantors Institute. He was also asked to join the faculty of Gratz College in Philadelphia, where he taught master classes in *nusah hatefillah*. Gratz presented him with an honorary doctorate in 1987. Max gave lectures in synagogues throughout the United States and Canada and also found time to write music, scholarly articles, and reviews.

Particularly interested in seeing that women could receive the diploma of *hazzan* from the Seminary, Max became their advocate, speaking to the issue throughout the country. The issue of women as rabbis had surfaced for full discussion by the faculty of the Seminary with the formation of the Commission for the Study of Ordination of Women as Rabbis. Chancellor Gerson Cohen (1924–91) had called the Commission into formation in October 1977, at the request of the Rabbinical Assembly of America. Cohen was asked to "study all aspects of the role of women as spiritual leaders in the Conservative movement." The Commission decided to limit itself to the question of whether women may or should be ordained as rabbis by the Rabbinical School of the Jewish Theological Seminary.

Public meetings were held in New York and throughout the country with representatives of the Commission listening to Conservative lay leaders as well as those in the general synagogue membership. These meetings were intended to explore the general attitude toward practice and acceptance of whatever decision lay in the future. The responses and suggestions of *amcha* (ordinary people) were to be taken into consideration by the commission. Gerson Cohen, who leaned toward keeping the status quo at the beginning of the lengthy and difficult discussions, was moved by the end of the process to an advocacy of women as rabbis.

The findings presented by the Commission to the 1979 convention of the Rabbinical Assembly were that "there is no direct halakhic objection to the acts of training and ordaining a woman to become a rabbi, preacher, and teacher in Israel" and that "it is morally wrong to maintain an educational structure that treats males and females equally up to the final stage, but distinguishes between them at that stage, without a firm and clearly identifiable halakhic reason for doing so."[46]

The Assembly decided to take no action and suggested that the Seminary faculty study the proposal and make a determination. Members of the faculty were asked to express their personal views. Eleven papers were written and distributed, of which nine, including majority and minority reports of the Commission, were eventually published.[47]

Concluding the response in favor of the issue is Joel Roth's (1940–) long defense and summation of the halakhic issues, which he thought entitled women to become rabbis if they accepted the *mitzvot* and the "status of obligation" upon themselves. Others on the faculty dissented, presenting their arguments in defense of the status quo. Still others argued for accepting women into the rabbinate without Roth's proviso.

At a 1980 meeting of the Executive Committee of the Cantors Assembly, speaking as a professor in the Cantors Institute and as one who had followed the progress of the question closely, Wohlberg gave a full report of the decision as well as the arguments and sources employed by both sides.

Cohen supported the policy change at the Seminary, but when the matter was brought to a faculty meeting in December 1979, the issue was so volatile, and the outcome so potentially destructive to the school, that it was tabled. At the Rabbinical Assembly convention in Dallas in April 1983, a vote for the admission to the Assembly of a woman, Rabbi Beverly Magidson (ordained at Hebrew Union College in 1979), barely missed the 75 percent requirement. This was a clear signal to the Seminary that action on the issue was now urgently required. It could no longer be avoided, no matter the consequence.

Once again, the debate raged in the Seminary halls and classrooms, but Chancellor Cohen was determined to bring conclusion to the issue. On October 24, 1983, the Seminary faculty voted 32–8 to admit women for ordination, a move of historic import and a profound change for the Seminary and the Conservative movement. According to Professor Neil Gillman (1933–   ), "The ordination of women is a landmark in the history of Conservative Judaism. It lent the movement the integrity it lacked for the better part of a century. In one stroke, it erased the inner tensions of the movement's founding ideology. Seminary, rabbinate, and lay community together had effectively affirmed that whatever else Torah is, it is also a cultural document, that it has always been and will continue to be affected by historical considerations, and that it is the Jewish community in every generation that serves as the authority for the ongoing shape of Judaism in matters of belief and practice."

It was inevitable that the admission of women to the Cantors Institute would follow the example of the Rabbinical School. Two women, Marla Barugel (1955–   ) and Erica Lippitz (1956–   ), were admitted to the program in 1983. Rabbi Amy Eilberg of Philadelphia, who had already completed most of the requirements as a student in the Graduate School, became the first woman ordained by the Seminary, in May 1985, and the Rabbinical Assembly, at its 1985 convention, admitted to its membership not only Rabbi Eilberg but also Rabbi Magidson and another reform graduate, Rabbi Jan Kaufman.

In January 1987, Chancellor Ismar Schorsch (1937–   ) announced that the Seminary would bestow its investiture as *hazzanim* upon Barugel and Lippitz. It was obvious that their graduation as *hazzanim* in May of that year would present the Cantors Assembly with a serious dilemma. In spite of the fact that the Cantors Assembly was required to accept graduates of the Cantors Institute as members (its by-laws mandated automatic acceptance of CI graduates as full members of the Assembly with all its privileges, including placement), the officers and board of the Assembly had failed to implement this article in spite of oral petitions to do so. Because this would precipitate a rift among the membership, the question of the admission of Barugel and Lippitz to the Assembly, with its plethora of Orthodox *hazzanim,* was held in abeyance by the Assembly for two years. But in 1990, a mandate for the acceptance of women *hazzanim* was prepared by the Executive Committee and presented to the membership of the Cantors Assembly at its national convention for a full vote.

It was to the credit of the Assembly that, in spite of voices raised on both sides, a general feeling of respect prevailed in what was a highly charged, emotional situation that was given much attention by the national press. There were extremists on both sides and innumerable private meetings to discuss strategies.

The small-statured Wohlberg, continually rising and speaking in favor of the mandate, often in rebuttal, did so in a calm, sensible, and effective manner. His attitude was often in marked contrast to the generally raucous and high-decibel arguments both for and against. Max would later remark that he "lost friends over this."

The vote was continually sidetracked and ambushed by those who had organized in opposition. Some against the admission of women spoke tearfully of their inability to even pray as *stam* (ordinary) Jews in a synagogue where the prayers were led by a female *hazzan.* Others threatened to resign or to form a new alliance in competition with the Assembly. After hours of discussion, the mandate was passed on a third stormy vote, much to the chagrin of the most traditional

Just as the right wing of the Conservative rabbis chose to leave the Rabbinical Assembly to form the Union for Traditional Judaism (originally, the Union for Traditional Conservative Judaism), so did a number of right-wing *hazzanim,* mostly from Canada, bolt from the Cantors Assembly to join the same organization as their traditional-minded rabbinic colleagues.

Max welcomed the women students, encouraging them in the same manner as he did their male counterparts. When he set about studying the women's vocal requirements for the performance of recitatives and other involvements in their preparation for service to the community, he decided that most of the recitatives written for high, male cantorial voice were inappropriate for sopranos and that settings in a lower range were more appropriate. The informal, weekly *nusah* presentations as well as the more formal recitals presented by male and female students in the cantorial school of the Seminary have more than borne out Max's assessment regarding range limitations for female cantors with soprano voices. If the tessitura (general range of pitch) of recitative settings is high and they are sung by a soprano, the ear seems to tire quickly and soon hears the sound as strident, loud, unsettling, or, in some cases, ugly. For some acoustical reason, the same passages sung by a tenor are listened to with interest. Until recently, recitatives had only been written for male voices, both in tenor and baritone keys. Unlike the sacred arias of J. S. Bach and other examples of the genre—where there is vocal relief of sorts in smooth and connected coloratura, dipping to lower pitches, as well as instrumental pauses with rest for the voice—cantorial recitatives often demand a consistently high tessitura, constant production of sound, and, depending on the composer, a difficult embellishment scheme. High-pitched coloratura sung by a soprano, unless sung smoothly and lightly, often sounds ludicrous. Among the solutions suggested by the faculty to female students at the Seminary are: avoid series of consistently high tones; approach high notes with caution and not at an extreme forte (loud); and generally, sing solo recitatives in a lower key. Contraltos and mezzo-sopranos do not have the same aesthetic problem.

On February 20, 1983, Max married Rochelle Myers. Max and Rochelle continued to be regular *shul*-goers, alternating between her Reform Congregation Beth Torah in northeast Philadelphia on Friday evenings and Max's Conservative synagogue, Adath Jeshurun in Elkins Park, on Saturday mornings and holidays. The circuit of synagogues in the Wohlberg prayer orbit increased yet further when Max's son, Jeffrey, became rabbi of Adas Israel Congregation in Washington, D.C.

Max's creative life continued unabated. He wrote choral pieces for the Cantors Institute chorus and conductor Matti Lazar (1947–), as well as for the chorus of the Philadelphia region of the Cantors Assembly, led by Cantor David Tilman (1944–).

Invitations for Max to be a guest speaker and lecturer continued as well. It was not uncommon for him to fly from one end of the country to the other on consecutive weekends, speaking on subjects as diverse as music, superstitions, humor, Yiddish song, and women in the Bible. Max spoke well, with humor and authority.

In spite of his age, Max still sang well and continued to substitute for other *hazzanim*. Leading services in Orlando, Florida, as he approached his eightieth birthday, it was evident that Max had lost none of his subtle humor. Approached by an elderly man at the conclusion of Yom Kippur who asked why Max never looked at the prayer book, Max impishly implored the congregant to keep his secret: "I need this job; don't tell the president, but I've never learned to read Hebrew—I memorize everything." He also served as *hazzan* with choir and organ during the High Holy Days at the 92nd Street Y in New York from 1981 to 1984.

On October 14, 1987, Max assumed the position of the first endowed chair at the Cantors Institute. At a luncheon, Ismar Schorsch, the newly installed chancellor of the Seminary, named him the Nathan Cummings Professor in Liturgy and *Hazzanut*. On November 1, 1987, the American Society for Jewish Music and the Cantors Institute of the Seminary, in cooperation with the American Conference of Cantors, the Leo Baeck Institute, and the Cantors Assembly of America, honored Max, together with musicologists Eric Werner and Albert Weisser (in memoriam).

As he approached his eighty-fourth birthday, Max was asked to reflect upon his own heroes:

> Throughout my life, I have held three men as my ideals: Pinchas Minkowski, the Russian *hazzan,* scholar, and author; Eduard Birnbaum [1855–1920], the musicologist, bibliographer of Jewish music, and *hazzan* who succeeded Hirsch Weintraub in Königsberg; and Abraham Zvi Idelsohn [1882–1938], the father of modern Jewish musicological research. Minkowski was my hero because of his vast knowledge and mastery of Russian, German, and Hebrew sources of Jewish music as well as for the idealism he brought to the profession and the disregard he showed with such vigor for what he considered to be vulgar or improper to the sacred calling of *hazzanut.* I held Birnbaum in the highest esteem because of the scholarship and single-mindedness he brought to the task of collecting the vast amount of materials known as the Birnbaum Collection, now incorporated into the library of the Hebrew Union College in Cincinnati. I idolized Idelsohn because of his great erudition and his achievements in breaking new ground for the scientific study and popularization of Jewish musicology in his monumental and outstanding works, as yet unsurpassed in scholarship and content, namely, the monumental *Thesaurus of Hebrew-Oriental Melodies* [1914–33], as well as others.[18]

In the lives of these three men, Wohlberg saw the essence of his own intellectual pursuits refined and saw their achievements as goals for him to strive for. Indeed, Wohlberg brought to the creation of Jewish music his own unique experiences, perceptions, and visions, generated in the shtetls and *yeshivot* of Hungary and refined through the culture of his adopted country. His accomplishments are precious and important as contributions of a unique American *hazzan*. He characterized the ideal *hazzan* as

> one who knows everything about Jewish music and is completely familiar with general music; one who knows the prayer book in its entirety as well as its history and the development of the prayers; one who knows the place of *nusah hatefillah* in all its aspects and who is able to use that knowledge for the creation of new forms of Jewish musical expression; and one who is able to use his abilities in the service of the Almighty.[19]

Max's health declined, and in March 1992, he moved to Washington, D.C., where he lived with Jeffrey, daughter-in-law Judy, and their children: Adam (1966–), Rachel (1969–), and Jeremy (1970–). He soon made good friends in Jeffrey's congregation and continued to attend synagogue on Shabbat and the holidays. Max became known as a reliable resource for the synagogue's study program and was active in the congregational community. His last musical work was written in honor of Jerusalem's three-thousandth anniversary year: *Yerushalayim, Yerushalayim* was a compilation of fifteen biblical references to Jerusalem, written for piano, solo voice, and male chorus. Arranged by this writer, the piece was premiered in Israel in August 1996 at the Cantors Assembly convention.

He took great pride in his grandchildren and was present at the Jewish Theological Seminary when grandson Adam was ordained as a rabbi; he also saw the graduation of granddaughter Rachel as a physician and was proud of grandson Jeremy's entrance into graduate school. A year before he died, Max again stepped in as an overflow cantor at Jeffrey's congregation, Adas Israel, for the High Holy Days. He sang with the fervor and nuances of which he was still a master, to the pleasure and amazement of the congregation.

Through a generous gift from Harvey Miller of Riverwoods, Illinois, Max's beloved Cantors Institute became the H. L. Miller Cantorial School of the Jewish Theological Seminary on March 26, 1996, with Rabbi Morton Leifman continuing as its long-serving dean. It was thus provided with a status equal to that of the other schools in the Seminary's complex. Max was too ill to attend the formal proceedings, but his contributions to its founding and development as well as the love that he had for the school and its students were suitably acknowledged. He died at home in Washington, D.C., surrounded by his family, on Rosh Hodesh Iyar, April 19, 1996. Following a funeral service at the Seminary, attended by faculty, scholars from the New York community, *hazzanim,* friends, and students, he was buried in the family plot in Elmont, on Long Island.

Tam venishlam: his book is completed.

A comment prompted by an exchange between Wohlberg and the author of an article in the *Jewish Spectator* that deprecated the role of the cantor and disparaged the state of choral music in the American synagogue:

As for my attitude to criticism of the cantorate, readers of this column know full well that self-criticism is its most frequent theme. Profanation of our profession and desecration of our sacred calling, from whatever source, have always been exposed within these lines. Lest I be misjudged, I will reiterate: the hazzan *is in great measure responsible for the musically chaotic, aesthetically insipid, and spiritually vapid state of our synagogue service. He is, however, not alone in guilt. When he transforms the prayer service into a concert performance . . . to exhibit the beauty and facility of his voice . . . [he] sows the seeds of spiritual decay. When congregations select* hazzanim *purely on the basis of vocal prowess . . . they then nurture the growth of a vicious weed. When rabbis accept ill-prepared, so-called cantors to serve in their pulpits, when they circumscribe and transform the service to a degree beyond the recognition of a regular worshiper, and when they dilute it with prosaic matters, they weaken a fundamental pillar and mitigate a pivotal element of traditional Judaism.*

—Wohlberg, Pirkei Hazzanut, *The Cantors Voice* 12, no. 1 (August 1961)

Notes

1. Joseph H. Levine, "Emunat Abba: The Early Years of Abba Weisgal, 1885–1921" (vol. 4, Ph.D. diss., Seminary College of Jewish Music, Jewish Theological Seminary, 1981), 16.
2. Ibid., 110.
3. From personal interviews that took place 1984–86.
4. Ibid.
5. Ibid.
6. Ibid.
7. Mark Slobin, *Chosen Voices: The Story of the American Cantorate* (Urbana and Chicago: University of Illinois Press, 1989), 64.
8. Personal interview.
9. Ibid.
10. Ibid.
11. Ibid.
12. Ibid.
13. Ibid.
14. A. Z. Idelsohn, *Jewish Music in Its Historical Development* (New York: Tudor Press, 1929; reissued, 1948), 205–16.
15. Slobin, 62.
16. Personal interview.
17. Personal letter from Joseph H. Levine, January 2000.
18. Personal interview.
19. Slobin, 57.
20. Personal interview.
21. Joseph H. Levine, "Psalmodic Chant of Abba Yosef Weisgal" (master's thesis, Cantors Institute of the Jewish Theological Seminary, 1979), 10.
22. Personal interview.
23. Ibid.
24. Slobin, 65.

25. Max Wohlberg, *Shirei Zimroh* (New York: Bloch, 1948).
26. Slobin, 62.
27. Personal interview.
28. Slobin, 65.
29. Ibid., 62.
30. Ibid.
31. Ibid., 66.
32. Personal interview.
33. Max Wohlberg, "Unique Chapter in the History of the American Cantorate," Journal of Synagogue Music 7, no. 1 (November 1976): 3.
34. Morton M. Leifman, "Max Wohlberg: Personal Memoir," *Journal of Synagogue Music* 7, no. 3 (June 1977): 33–34.
35. Personal interview.
36. Rabbi Paul Steinberg and Zelda Goldsmith, conversations and e-mail, July 22–25, 2000.
37. Edwin Wolf II and Maxwell Whiteman, *The History of the Jews in Philadelphia* (Philadelphia: Jewish Publication Society of America, 1957), 41.
38. Ibid., 372.
39. Ibid., 373.
40. Personal interview.
41. Slobin, 71–72.
42. Max Wohlberg, "Curriculum Guide for First-Year Students," ed. C. Davidson (New York: Cantors Institute of the Jewish Theological Seminary, 1978).
43. Ibid.
44. Mordecai Kaplan, address to United Synagogue, June 22, 1947.
45. Joseph H. Levine, *Synagogue Song in America* (Crown Point, Ind.: White Cliffs Media, 1989), 23.
46. Neil Gillman, *Conservative Judaism for the New Century* (New York: Behrman House, 1993), 133.
47. Simon Greenberg, ed., *The Ordination of Women as Rabbis: Studies and Responsa*, vol. 14, Moreshet Series (New York: Jewish Theological Seminary, 1988).
48. Personal correspondence, October 1987.
49. Ibid.

Photographs

Szatmar yeshiva students: (left to right) Harry, Max, Joseph, 1917.

20-year-old Cantor Max Wohlberg with his choir at the Gates Avenue Shul, Brooklyn, 1927. (brother Joseph at his right)

Hazzan and "Rabbi," College Point, Queens, 1929.

Portrait, 1930s.

Family Portrait, 1930s:
(left to right) Madeline, Max, Hermina, Harry, Jerome (Eckstein), Blanche (Eckstein), Mord'che (Eckstein), Joseph.

Teaching at the Cantors Institute, the Jewish Theological Seminary of America, 1950s.

Portrait, 1940s.

At the Seminary, 1970s.

Bidding farewell to A. Z. Idelsohn, who is returning to South Africa:
(left to right) Mrs. Idelsohn, Ephraim Spivack (*Hazzanim Farband*),
Max Wohlberg, Dr. Joseph Shapiro (Jewish Department, Library of Congress),
Louis Lippitz (*Hazzanim Farband*), Jacob Beimel, Gershon Ephros.

At Seminary graduation, 1990.

(left to right) Max Wohlberg, Charles Davidson, Rabbi Ya'akov G. Rosenberg, 1978.

Philadelphia Regional Branch of the Cantors Assembly, 1957.

Announcing the establishment of the Cantors Institute,
May 1952, Concord Hotel, Kiamesha Lake, New York
The Fifth Convention of the Cantors Assembly of America:
(left to right) Cantor Jacob Hohenemser, Cantor W. Belskin Ginsberg, Rabbi Max Davidson, Rabbi Max Routtenberg, Rabbi Moshe Davis, Cantor Abraham Rose.

Cantors Institute of the Jewish Theological Seminary, 1952
(left to right, seated) Faculty: Herman Berlinski, Siegfried Landau, Solomon Rosowsky, Marvin Wiener, Hugo Weisgall, Max Wohlberg, David Putterman
(left to right, standing) Students: Morton Shames, Paul Kavon, Robert Zalkin

Preparing for 1952 Cantors Assembly cantorial concert at Town Hall to raise funds for the Seminary's New Cantorial School:
(left to right) Organist George Crook, Conductor Siegfried Landau, and executive director of the Assembly, David Putterman

1980

Seminary granting honorary doctorate to Samuel Rosenbaum, executive director of the Cantors Assembly of America, 1990: (left to right) Rabbi Shammai Kanter, Vice Chancellor David Kogen, Cantor Max Wohlberg, Cantor Samuel Rosenbaum, Dean Morton Leifman

The Jewish Theological Seminary

Beth El Synagogue choir Minneapolis, May 19, 1942

Hazzanim Farband, circa 1930

It is true that all too many High Holy Day Jews are nonparticipants in the service and appear as noninterested listeners. Yet they must find emotional gratification and spiritual satisfaction being present at a religious service in the company of their fellow Jews. . . . Their emotional attachments to the religion of their fathers . . . was sufficient to overcome their serious lack of knowledge of fundamentals. Our task, therefore, it seems to me, is to increase instruction, but not at the price of reduced inspiration. Concurrently, we should endeavor to make every religious service spiritually edifying.

—Wohlberg, Pirkei Hazzanut, *The Cantors Voice* 11, no. 1 (February 1961)

Max Wohlberg Bibliography

Abbreviations

CV   *The Cantors Voice*
JMN *Jewish Music Notes*
JSM *Journal of Synagogue Music*
UJE *Universal Jewish Encyclopedia*

Biographical Articles

Bernstein, A. M. *Musikalisher Pinkas* (New York: Cantors Assembly of America, 1958; repr. of *A Collection of Zemirot and Folk Melodies,* compiled by A. M. Bernstein, Vilna, 1927). Foreword by Wohlberg, in which he describes the life and works of Bernstein: composer, *hazzan,* and collector of Hassidic and Yiddish tunes.

Ephros, Gershon. "To Gershon Ephros: In Lieu of a Kaddish," *JSM* 9, no. 1 (March 1979): 33–34. Wohlberg's eulogy to Ephros.

"Ephros, Gershon, 1890–1978," *JSM* 19, no. 2 (December 1989).

Glantz, Leib. Article by Wohlberg on Leib Glantz with comments on his recordings as well as review of "Ham'chadesh," by Eliezer Steinman, repr. of article in *Ha'aretz* (Tel Aviv: Tel Aviv Institute for Jewish Religious Music, 1965), 45–46. Wohlberg considers Glantz the most innovative of all *hazzanim.*

Glantz, Leib. "Leib Glantz, Zikhrono Liv'rakha: Hazzan He-Hazzanim," *Ha'aretz,* February 28, 1964. Obituary and tribute (Hebrew).

"Idelsohn, Abraham Zvi," *UJE* 5: 534–35. Idelsohn's work in its historical perspective. Comments on the adoption by Peter Wagner (a leading authority in plainsong) of Idelsohn's idea of Gregorian chant as a basis for Jewish music.

"Jassinowski, Pinchos," *UJE* 6: 42. *Hazzan,* composer, and author, Jassinowski was among the first to employ modern Yiddish poetry for his compositions and the first *hazzan* to sing on the radio (1923).

"Kwartin, Zavel," *UJE* 6: 494. Wohlberg is appreciative of Kwartin's "mellow . . . baritone."

"Lewandowski, Louis," *UJE* 7: 20–21. Biography of the composer, choir director, and teacher.

"Lowy, Israel," *UJE* 7: 220–21. Wohlberg states that "as a result of the great crowds storming the synagogue whenever [Lowy] officiated, the Jewish *Kehillah* of Paris decided to build a larger synagogue with an organ."

"Minkowski, Pinchas," *UJE* 7: 570–71. Wohlberg attributes the modernization of the Broder Synagogue in Odessa to Minkowski and Nowakowski.

"Naumbourg, Samuel," *UJE* 8: 132–33. Biography including Naumbourg's formulation of a unified service for all French synagogues.

"Roitman, David," *UJE* 9: 183. Biography and commentary that Roitman's compositions are in the style of Eastern Europe and "permeated with the sad fate of the Jewish people."

"Rosenblatt, Josef," *UJE* 9: 210. Biography and observation that "Rosenblatt was the most beloved *hazzan* of his age, his name becoming as well known as that of Caruso."

"Rozowski, Baruch Leib," *UJE* 9: 267–68. Biography of the "*hazzan*, composer, and Hebrew scholar, the first Jew accepted to the conservatory of Saint Petersburg."

"Schlesinger, Sigmund," *UJE* 9: 409. Biography of the "composer, cantor, organist, and choirmaster of Sha'arei Shomayim in Mobile, Alabama, whose melodies were among the first to be published in America for Reform temples."

"Schorr, Boruch," *UJE* 9: 423. Schorr had a "powerful and flexible voice" and wrote "dramatic and interpretive compositions, achieving unique effects of . . . instrumental color" with his choir.

"Schwartz, Jacob," *UJE* 9: 423. Biography of the *hazzan*-composer who founded the Cantor Schwartz Institute of *Hazzanut* in 1915.

"Singer, Josef," *UJE* 9: 556. Succeeded Sulzer in Vienna and "was among the first to give *hazzanut* a scientific foundation."

"Sparger, William," *UJE* 9: 691. Collaborator with Max Spicker in early works for the American Reform synagogue.

"Straschunsky, Joel David," *UJE* 10: 74. Biography of the Vilner *Balabeisel*.

"Sulzer, Solomon," *UJE* 10: 101–2. Observations on "the father of modern synagogue music."

Sulzer, Solomon. "Solomon Sulzer and the *Seitenstettengasse* Temple," *JSM* 2, no. 4 (April 1970): 19–24. Biography and assessment of the famous "*Kantor*" and his contribution to Jewish music.

Sulzer, Solomon. "Vienna's Most Honored Singer," *Jewish Spectator* 35, no. 2 (February 1970): 20–21. Sulzer's musical contribution to synagogue music, which "remains unequalled to this day."

Weisser, Joshua S. *Shirei Beth Hakeneseth*, vol. 2, for the High Holy Days (New York:

Metro Music, 1952). Introduction by Wohlberg, in which he states musical background and evaluates the work of Weisser, whom he calls "outstanding and the most prolific" of the European-born *hazzanim*. Commenting on Weisser's large output, Wohlberg applauds the use of "tradition, *nusah*, utility, and variety."

Weisser, Joshua S. Pirkei Hazzanut, *CV* 5, no. 1 (September 1952): 2, 7. Biography of Joshua S. Weisser and review of his works.

Wohlberg, Max. "Pirkei Hazzanut," *JSM* 1, no. 3 (January 1968): 49–52. Autobiographical remarks about Wohlberg's early years in America.

"Zilberts, Zavel," *UJE* 10: 643. Biography of the composer and choral conductor.

Pirkei Hazzanut, *CV* 10, no. 1 (February 1959): 2, 12. Laudations to Mark Silver, Henry Lefkowitz, and Lazar Weiner.

April 18 is the anniversary of one of the most glorious yet tragic episodes in our long history. A deceived, suppressed, persecuted, starved, humiliated, submissive, and peace-loving, unarmed minority resolved to resist the most powerful, most cruel, and sadistic military machine, in the full realization that it would perish in the effort. This heroic event appears in even more majestic aspect when compared with the most evil and brutal, mortally corrupt regime in the history of our so-called civilization. While Warsaw was no exception in its sad fate, it was singled out by the Nazis as the ultimate depot and infamous Umschlagplatz on the way to the Final Solution. Warsaw, it must be recalled, was one of the most active Jewish centers in the world. In the realm of scholarship, culture, music, and the arts, it was preeminent. Its numerous synagogues, particularly the four largest—Tlomackie, Nozhik, Sinai, Moriah—were served by the world's most distinguished hazzanim. *Among these were M. Hast, Jacob Weiss, R. Y. Rabinowitch, G. Sirota, A. Elfand, E. Zaludkowsky, P. Sherman, A. Katchko, M. Koussevitsky, and J. Eidelson. Its celebrated choral conductors included L. Low, D. Eisenstadt (Tlomackie), A. Davidowitch (Nozhik), M. Guttwerk (Sinai), M. Shneir, and M. Boaz. From all sources, it seems that the revolt in the Ghetto lasted approximately two months while all Poland fell in twenty-six days. Bernard Goldstein, a survivor and author, wrote: "I looked around me at what had been the Jews of Warsaw. May this sea of emptiness bubble and boil, may it cry out eternal condemnation of the murderers and pillagers, may it forever be the shame of the civilized world that saw and heard and chose to remain silent."*

—Wohlberg, Pirkei Hazzanut, *The Cantors Voice* 13, no. 3 (April 1963)

Articles on Jewish Music

"An Analysis of the Minor Modes," in *Proceedings of the 17th Annual Convention of the Cantors Assembly of America* (May 24–28, 1964), 24–29. Inherent relationships between cantillation and aspects of synagogue motives. Musical illustrations from Wohlberg, Baer, and Idelsohn.

"The Cantorate: Pages from Its History," in *The Cantorial Art* (New York: National Jewish Music Council, 1966), 11–33. Cantors' contributions to the music of the synagogue with a historical sketch of the profession itself.

"In der Chazanim Kultur Organizatsia," *Die Shul un Chazanim Welt,* no. 54 (August 1939, final issue). Activities and programs in the Cantors Ministers Cultural Organization.

"The Contributions of East European Jewry to the Music of the Synagogue," in *The Historic Contribution of Russian Jewry to Jewish Music,* ed. Irene Heskes and Arthur Wolfson (New York: National Jewish Music Council, 1967), 1–7. Those from Russia and Poland who contributed to the music of the synagogue from 1825 to 1925.

"The Emerging Image of the Conservative Cantor," *JSM* 7, no. 3 (June 1977): 17–20. Convocation address of May 1977, addressing the change of cantorial function from that of "weekend performer to *sheliah tzibbur.*"

"Exchange of Letters between Professors Weisser and Wohlberg," *JSM* 6, no. 2 (October 1975): 61–64. Albert Weisser questions Wohlberg on his statement that there is a "Jewish preference for violin over piano" ("Varying Concepts of *Ne'imah* and Their Place in the Liturgy," *JSM* 5, no. 3 [December 1974]).

"Folk Songs," *UJE* 4: 350–55. From Europe, Palestine, and the United States, mostly music and texts in Yiddish, nineteenth and twentieth centuries.

Foreword to *T'hillah V'zimrah* (New York: Cantors Assembly of America, 1958; repr. of works by A. S. Ersler, Wloclawek, 1907). Discussion of three groups of synagogue composers who followed Sulzer: Western (Lewandowski and Eduard Birnbaum); Eastern (Gerowitch and A. B. Birnbaum); and a heterogeneous group (Belzer, Rovner, and others).

"*Hazzanut* in Retrospect," *CV* 1, no. 5 (April 1949): 3. The "Golden Age of *Hazzanut*" (1800–1949) in review.

"*Hazzanut* in Transition," *JSM* 7, no. 3 (July 1977): 5–16. Development of *hazzanut* from talmudic times until today.

"The History of the Musical Modes of the Ashkenazic Synagogue and Their Usage," *JSM* 4, nos. 1–2 (April 1972): 46–61. Comments on early analyses of the Jewish musical modes; includes responses by Glantz and Yasser to Wohlberg's critique of their approach.

"Music and Musicians in the Works of Sholom Aleichem," *JSM* 6, no. 1 (April 1975): 20–42. Excerpts from Sholom Aleichem's works referring to music or musicians.

"Music of the Rosh Hashanah Liturgy," in *Rosh Hashanah Anthology*, ed. Philip Goodman (Philadelphia: Jewish Publication Society of America, 1970), 171–84. Rosh Hashanah melodies used by Ashkenazic Jews.

"Music of the Synagogue," lecture (New York: National Jewish Music Council, April 1957). Also in Spanish. Historical account of the history of Jewish music, with illustrations.

"Music of the Synagogue as a Source of the Yiddish Folk Song," *Musica Judaica* 2, no. 1 (1977–78): 21–49. Wohlberg furthers Idelsohn's work in identifying synagogal influences on Yiddish folk songs.

"Music of the Yom Kippur Liturgy," in *Yom Kippur Anthology*, ed. Philip Goodman (Philadelphia: Jewish Publication Society of America, 1971), 99–112. Melodies sung by Ashkenazic Jews on Yom Kippur.

"Nusah Notes," *JSM* 21, no. 2 (December 1991): 25–32. Wohlberg quotes a major motive found at the conclusion of the Shabbat *Avot* and finds it reflected in *brit milah*, festival, and High Holy Day prayers.

"Prayer and Music: A Rejoinder," *Conservative Judaism* 22, no. 2 (winter 1968): 73–76. Response to Jack Gottlieb's article in same issue on editing music.

Pirkei Hazzanut, *CV* 6, no. 2 (February 1954): 2. Examination of types of Hassidic tunes and their evaluation as appropriate for inclusion in the synagogue service.

Pirkei Hazzanut, *CV* 6, no. 3 (May 1954): 2. Remarks about famous *hazzanim* of the past and a call for further historical research.

Pirkei Hazzanut, *CV* 13, no. 3 (April 1963): 2, 9. Article on the occasion of the twentieth anniversary of the uprising of the Warsaw Ghetto; Poland as a source of distinguished *hazzanim*.

"Der Progress fun der Chazanim Kultur Organizatsia," *Die Shul un Chazanim Welt*, no. 52 (June 1939). Report of the activities of the short-lived predecessor of the Cantors Assembly of America (Yiddish).

"Purim Kaddish," *JSM* 8, no. 2 (May 1978): 21–27. Historical review of Purim customs and a setting of a Purim *Kaddish*.

Routtenberg, Lilly S., and Ruth R. Selden, *The Jewish Wedding Book* (New York:

Schocken, 1968), 115–16. Wohlberg's contribution to the volume is a list of suitable music for the marriage ceremony.

"Synagogue Music Published in the 19th and 20th Centuries," *UJE* 8: 54–55. Fifty-six musical suggestions for use in Orthodox, Reform, and Conservative services.

"Unique Chapter in the History of the American Cantorate," *JSM* 7, no. 1 (November 1976): 3–25. One year's minutes of meetings of the *Hazzanim Farband*, which became the Cantors Ministers Cultural Organization (1938) [appendix D in this volume].

"Unique Chapter in the History of the American Cantorate," *JSM* 7, no. 2 (February 1977): 3–15. Part 2 of the record of "a short-lived attempt . . . to refashion the character of the cantorate in America" [appendix D in this volume].

"Variations in *Nusah*," *CV* 1, no. 1 (May 1948): 2. Analysis of the music of the Ashkenazic synagogue, stating that there are few extant variations.

"Variations in *Nusah*," *CV* 1, no. 2 (June 1948): 2. Continuation with inclusion of variations between Eastern and Western European traditions.

"Varying Concepts of *Ne'imah* and Their Place in the Liturgy," *JSM* 5, no. 3 (December 1974): 16–21. Exposition on the word in "diverse grammatical forms with its varying concepts of pleasantness and melody."

"V'shir E'erach L'kha-B'nigun Un'imah (R. Yitzhak Luria)," introduction to *Yalkut Z'mirotai, (Shabbat Z'mirot)* composed by Wohlberg (Elkins Park, Pa.: Ashbourne Music, 1981). References cited to explain "the origin, history and traditional place of *Shabbat Z'mirot* in Jewish life."

Considering the qualities and estimating the contributions of the world-renowned cantors of the current century, one cannot but conclude that, although most of them shared some gifts, each was distinguished by other specific and individual characteristics. Thus, Karniol excelled with a voice of wide range and with fluid coloratura; Rosenblatt with an elastic and warm voice, with captivating tunefulness and with a remarkably facile falsetto; Kwartin with a perfectly placed voice, effortless coloratura, and an unaffected, techina-*like plaintive style; Hershman with a beautiful, mellow tenor and lyric-romantic delivery; Roitman with ecstasy and with effervescent spirit; Shteinberg with unassuming grace and folksy charm; Sirota with a brilliant and powerful Heldentenor and with fiery temperament; Minkowski with fine production; Pinchik with mystical piety and Hassidic fervor; the Koussevitsky brothers with phenomenal vocal virtuosity; and with Gantchoff, Brinn, and Vigoda, unmistakably individual styles. . . . Glantz . . . with a unique and original approach to* hazzanut *with a light, pliant, lyric tenor, employed with remarkable dexterity. . . . He concentrates on the meaning of every prayer and endeavors to find hidden significance and subtle interpretation in every liturgical text.*

—Wohlberg, "Leib Glantz: The Innovator," *The Cantors Voice* 14, no. 3 (April 1964)

CRITICAL REVIEWS

"Five Jewish Art Songs, by Lazar Weiner," *CV* 12, no. 2 (December 1961): 7. Wohlberg refers to these songs as "among the finest in our musical literature."

Legendary Voices, Samuel Vigoda, *JSM* 12, no. 2 (December 1982). Biographies cover fact and fiction.

"Moshe Nathanson: Singer, Composer, Teacher," *JWB Circle,* Jewish Bookland section (March 1974): 3. A review of *Song Without Words: The Life of Israel's Sweetest Singer: Moshe Nathanson* by Sheldon Feinberg; Wohlberg recalls that Nathanson sang "on the concert stage, records, and radio with great success and authenticity, the songs of reborn Israel."

"Music for Jewish Weddings," *JMN* (fall 1965): 1–2. Discussion of an article by Charles Davidson and Sholom Secunda. Wohlberg includes a list of appropriate music compiled by Davidson.

"Music of the Sephardim," *JMN* (winter 1961): 2 (also in *Le Judaïsme Sephardi, Organe de la Fédération Sephardité,* Mondiale, Nouvelle Serie, no. 24 [London, 1962]). A historical approach to reviews of newly published books and recordings.

"Notes on Music, Old and New," *JSM* 3, no. 2 (February 1971): 15–19. Condemns the illegal practice of reproducing music, praises the Cantors Assembly for publishing out-of-print volumes as well as new music, and cites the publications of Zavel Zilberts, Todros Greenberg, Israel Alter, Salomon Rossi, and Issachar Fater.

Pirkei Hazzanut, *CV* 2, no. 4 (January 1951). A review of *Toldos Haneginoh Vehachazonus* by Hyman H. Harris, praising it as the first anthology of its kind written in Hebrew.

Pirkei Hazzanut, *CV* 2, no. 5 (March 1951): 1. A review of *Encyclopedia Le Musika: A Biographical Dictionary of Jewish and World Musicians* by Israel Shalita, commenting that the section devoted to *hazzanut* is unwarrantedly skimpy but lauds the portion devoted to Israeli composers.

Pirkei Hazzanut, *CV* 2, no. 6 (June 1951): 1. Comments on the secular music, poetry, and liturgical compositions of Pinchos Jassinowski.

Pirkei Hazzanut, *CV* 4, no. 1 (November 1951): 2. A review of Joshua S. Weisser's *Shirei Beth Hakeneseth;* Wohlberg calls Weisser "the most popular, prolific, and utilitarian composer of our own day."

Pirkei Hazzanut, *CV* 4, no. 2 (January 1952): 2, 6. A mixed review of Alfred Sendrey's *Bibliography of Jewish Music.*

Pirkei Hazzanut, *CV* 4, no. 3 (March 1952): 2, 7. A tribute to Abraham Z. Idelsohn and a review of the third edition of his *Jewish Song Book.*

Pirkei Hazzanut, *CV* 5, no. 2 (December 1952): 2, 9. The problems of: (1) composing new Jewish music vs. the use of traditional *nusah;* (2) proper harmonization of the modes. Article centers on Gershon Ephros, who "fuses the old and new in his *Cantorial Anthology.*"

Pirkei Hazzanut, *CV* 6, no. 1 (October 1953): 2, 6. Hassidic song and the works of M. S. Geshuri.

Pirkei Hazzanut, *CV* 7, no. 2 (April 1955): 2. Review of recording issued by Hyman H. Harris, chanting the Eastern European *hazzanut* of the High Holy Days and *Selihot.*

Pirkei Hazzanut, *CV* 13, no. 2 (January 1963): 2, 6. Examination of the *Weekday Prayer Book* (Rabbinical Assembly of America), pointing out its shortcomings.

Pirkei Hazzanut, *CV* 15, no. 4 (June 1965): 2, 12. Reviews of *Amudei Ha'abodah* ("an indispensable book for anyone wishing to know the sources of our *piyyutim, z'mirot, s'lihot, kinot*") and *The Architecture of the European Synagogue.* Reviewed also is the television production of "Terezin Requiem." Discusses meeting with a survivor of the Terezin Ghetto.

Pirkei Hazzanut, *CV* 16, no. 2 (May 1966): 2. Discusses poor taste of commercial advertisements that fail to distinguish between the mundane and the religious aspects of a Jewish festival. Praise for Cantor Abraham Brun, survivor of the Lodz Ghetto.

Pirkei Hazzanut, *JSM* 13, no. 1 (June 1983): 30–31. A review of *Shiron Chadash,* a music book by Gershon Ephros.

"The Prayers of David . . . Are Ended, Ps. 72:20," *JSM* 10, no. 1 (July 1980): 3–9. Tribute to David Putterman and review of *Mizmor L'David.*

Recent Books, *JMN* (spring 1957): 2. Review of Reuben R. Rinder's *Music and Prayer.*

"Review of the *Concise Code of Jewish Law,* by Rabbi Gerson Appel," *JSM* 8, no. 2 (May 1978): 37–38.

"Seder Service," *JMN* (spring 1957). Review of the recording *A Passover Seder with Jan Peerce* (includes music of Ario S. Hyams).

"*Shabbat at Home* Recording Praised," *JMN* (winter 1964): 1–2. Review of the recording produced by the Women's League of the United Synagogue of America.

"Some Thoughts on the Hazzanic Recitative," *JSM* 9, no. 3 (November 1979): 82–86. Review of Noach Schall's *Hazzanic Thesaurus: Sabbath.*

The Songs We Sing, selected and edited by Harry Coopersmith, reviewed by Wohlberg in "An Artistic Achievement," *The Rabbinical Assembly of America Bulletin* 1, no. 4 (April 1950): 3. Wohlberg calls it "the greatest step forward on the road to finer Jewish music for school and for the home."

"*The Songs We Sing,* by Harry Coopersmith," *CV* 2, no. 2 (June 1950): 4. In spite of flaws, "the greatest step forward."

Studies in Jewish Music: The Collected Works of A. W. Binder, ed. Irene Heskes. Reviewed by Wohlberg in *JMN* (summer 1972): 2.

"The Subject of Jewish Music: A Review of Nulman's *Concise Encyclopedia of Jewish Music,*" *JSM* 6, no. 2 (October 1975): 44–50. "Errors of omission, commission, and faulty scholarship."

―――――∽∼―――――

It seems incongruous that cantillation, in all likelihood the most ancient element of Jewish music, was for the first time transcribed into musical notation by a priest, Johann Boschenstein, in the Hebrew grammar of Johannes Reuchlin, Hagenau, 1518, and then left in the province of non-musicians. While the grammatical aspects of the system of cantillation were fairly well attended to, its musical ingredients, until our generation, were, with but one exception, shabbily neglected. Abraham Baer, with the painstaking effort shown throughout his Ba'al Tefillah, *endeavored to compile a list of cantillations from comparative versions of the tropes. The subject, however, was treated cavalierly by practically everyone else. Happily, a change took place in our day. Following the footsteps of S. Rosowsky (*The Cantillation of the Bible*), Y. L. Ne'eman (*Tseliley Hammiqra*) and A. W. Binder (*Biblical Chant*) produced thoroughly competent books on the subject. Pinchas Spiro, an eminently qualified* hazzan *and educator, aware of the need for a practical cantillation textbook . . . devoted mainly to the chant of the Haftarah and the Torah, succeeded in producing a volume (*Haftarah Chanting*) that is well planned . . . and sensibly executed.*

—Wohlberg, review of *Haftarah Chanting, The Cantors Voice* 15, no. 3 (March 1965)

―――――∽∼―――――

Essays

"Bar Mitzvah Instruction," *The Synagogue School* 12, no. 1 (September 1953): 3–10. Wohlberg deals with the preparation of the bar mitzvah, particularly with the teaching of cantillation. He suggests materials, discusses time allotted for instruction, methods, classroom equipment, and the teaching of *maftir, Kiddush,* and *Yigdal.*

"*Beiti—Beit Tefillah,*" *Conservative Judaism* 13, no. 3 (spring 1959): 27–36. Personal philosophy regarding worship, the liturgy, congregants, *hazzan,* synagogue composer, and music used in the synagogue service [appears in this volume as appendix B].

"Elements to Consider When Composing Synagogue Music," *JSM* 24, no. 2 (December 1995): 5–12. From the viewpoint of congregant and composer.

"Fading Footprints," *JSM* 6, no. 4 (July 1976): 21–26. Tribute paid to *hazzanim,* musicians of the Holocaust.

"The *Hazzan* as Spokesman of the Congregation," *JSM* 20, no. 2 (December 1990): 28–32. Traditional commentaries on the issue.

"Jewish Musical Creativity in America," *CV* 10, no. 1 (February 1959): 5. Progress report on advances in Jewish music by Americans.

"Musical Tasks for the Future," *Jewish Liturgical Music Society of America,* no. 1 (September 1963): 1. New compositions based upon older music; education to fight apathy and indifference toward Jewish music; creating a *nusah Yisra'el.*

"My Impressions of Synagogal Services in Israel and Europe," in *Proceedings of the 11th Annual Conference-Convention of the Cantors Assembly and the Department of Music of the United Synagogue of America* (April 21, 1958). Concludes with the prediction that if synagogue music is to develop at all, it will do so in the United States.

Pirkei Hazzanut, *CV* 5, no. 3 (April 1953): 2, 6. Rails against carelessness in attributing authorship of compositions.

Pirkei Hazzanut, *CV* 7, no. 1 (December 1954): 2. A list of sins of omission on behalf of *hazzanim.*

Pirkei Hazzanut, *CV* 8, no. 1 (March 1956): 2. The building of new synagogues and the place of liturgical music.

Pirkei Hazzanut, *CV* 9, no. 1 (November 1957): 2. Calls for the formation of *shomrei nusha'ot* to safeguard tradition; laments the omission of liturgical portions in the service.

Pirkei Hazzanut, *CV* 9, no. 2 (February 1958): 2. Suggests adding time to the beginning of the service.

Pirkei Hazzanut, *CV* 11, no. 1 (February 1961): 2, 8. Disagrees with Trude Weiss-Rosmarin's suggestion that High Holy Day services be shortened and the time saved devoted to lectures and discussions.

Pirkei Hazzanut, *CV* 11, no. 2 (May 1961): 2, 6. Four questions in the spirit of the Passover season: (1) How to replace old, cherished tunes with new ones; (2) How to keep the distinguishing elements of *nusah hatefillah* extant; (3) How to remember the Holocaust in prayer; (4) How to reflect the Land of Israel in our worship.

Pirkei Hazzanut, *CV* 12, no. 1 (August 1961): 2, 7. Decries "musically chaotic, aesthetically insipid, and spiritually vapid state of our synagogue service" and blames cantors, rabbis, and congregations.

Pirkei Hazzanut, *CV* 12, no. 2 (December 1961): 2, 8. Calls for a Jewish musical periodical.

Pirkei Hazzanut, *CV* 12, no. 3 (March 1962): 2, 8. Defends *hazzanim* against excessive and unjustified accusations, e.g., cantors accused by rabbis of being "high-priced warblers," "singing too much," and "disgusted that a cantor's status would be equated to that of a rabbi." Wohlberg also disapproves of a photograph of a cantor dressed in vestments, advertising a concert on a poster in a Chinese restaurant.

Pirkei Hazzanut, *CV* 12 [*sic;* should be 13], no. 1 (September 1962): 2, 12. Calls for composers to combine the distinctive features of Ashkenazic and Sephardic music.

Pirkei Hazzanut, *CV* 14, no. 1 (September 1963): 2, 12. Bidding farewell to the regular appearance of his column with this issue of the *Cantors Voice*. Lists topics that *hazzanim* might lecture on as well as names and dates of old-time *hazzanim*.

Pirkei Hazzanut, *CV* 17, no. 1 (September 1966): 23–24. Defends the *hazzan's* right to perform marriages as well as his right to tax-exempt parsonage allowance.

Pirkei Hazzanut, *JSM* 1, no. 1 (February 1967): 57–59. Wohlberg's first cantorial positions and his recollections of a tape recording of his father's singing.

"Prayer and Music: A Rejoinder," *Conservative Judaism* 22, no. 2 (winter 1968): 73–76. Ways to revitalize Jewish music.

"*Shiru Lo,*" *Conservative Judaism* 23, no. 1 (fall 1968): 60–66. Congregational participation as evidenced in the Bible and Talmud and its current development and practice [appears in this volume as appendix C].

"Sing Unto the Lord: Toward a New Congregational Chant," in *Community and Cul-*

ture: Essays in Jewish Studies in Honor of the Ninetieth Anniversary of the Founding of Gratz College, ed. Nahum M. Waldman (Philadelphia: Seth Press, 1987), 243–48.

"Transylvania," *UJE* 10: 295–96. History of the Jewish communities of Transylvania until 1942.

"What Does the Cantor Expect of His Congregation and Rabbi?" *Proceedings of the 1st Annual Conference-Convention of the Cantors Assembly and the Department of Music of the United Synagogue of America* (New York: February 10–12, 1948), 18–20. Wohlberg asks for respect, job security, and authority in the area of music in the synagogue for the Conservative *hazzan*.

"Wider Horizons for Jewish Liturgical Music," *JMN* (spring 1963): 1–2. Composition, education, musicology. Calls for the inclusion of Sephardic motives.

Custom decrees that before the month of Tishri, the Yehi Rotzon *for* Rosh Hodesh *is omitted. This is indeed regrettable. For the prayer for life without shame* (she'ein bohem bushoh) *is for us* hazzanim *never more pertinent than before the High Holy Days, when the embarrassingly vulgar (particularly in Yiddish) newspaper ads raucously proclaim the exaggerated claims and the artistic merits of* shelihei tzibbur. *How these ostentatious and boastful references to faultless voice, to mastery of improvisation, to perfection of* nusah *and to unsurpassed excellence can be reconciled with the affirmations of the* Hineni *and with the simile of* heres hanishbor *is beyond me. What I find particularly disturbing, in addition to the vulgarity in taste, is the impropriety of spiritual functionaries adopting the attitude of strutting peacocks, publicly preening their conceit without shame and without a trace of embarrassment. This display of insensitive—often self-composed—ballyhoo must be most painful to anyone to whom public prayer is a sincere religious experience and to those who consider the* hazzan *a religious functionary.*

—Wohlberg, Pirkei Hazzanut, *The Cantors Voice* 16, no. 2 (May 1966)

Unpublished Articles

"Answering *Amen* after the Blessing *Ga'al Yisra'el*." Response to Professor Weiss-Halivni on the appropriateness of an audible "amen" following the aforementioned *brakha*. Wohlberg is in favor of it.

"Basic Library of a *Hazzan*." Paper prepared for Seminary College of Jewish Music, Cantors Institute, Extension Department, 1965. Lists prayer books (13), liturgical source books (13), source books for law and custom (11), sources for *nusah* (9), compilations for cantor and choir (20), recitative collections (11), books for congregational singing (8), song collections (5), *zemirot* collections (6), collections of Israeli songs (11), songs for younger children (4), sources for Jewish musicology (27), and more.

"A Comparative Study of Weekday *Nusah*." Lecture presented at a joint all-day conference of *hazzanim* and students of the Cantors Institute of the Jewish Theological Seminary, December 1968. Motifs based on tropal signs and their differences in the Ashkenazic tradition were analyzed and demonstrated.

"From Eve to Golda and Beyond." A narrative script about women in the Bible, with musical illustrations in English for solo voice (August 1975).

"The Harmonization of the Music of the Synagogue." Paper written at the request of Joseph Yasser. Wohlberg reviews music of the Ashkenazic synagogue.

"Modes Most Frequently Encountered in the Ashkenazic Liturgy." Prepared for students of the Cantors Institute and the Seminary College of Jewish Music of the Jewish Theological Seminary, October 10, 1961.

"Study on the Fundamental Aspects of the Ashkenazic *Hazzanic* Recitatives." Paper presented at the International Congress of Jewish Music, Israel, 1978. Analyses and forty musical examples.

APPENDIX A
Max Wohlberg Family Tree

Great-great-grandfather was Ya'akov Wohlberg (1700s);
his son was Israel Shlomo.

Great-grandfather was Israel Shlomo, who had five sons and two daughters;
his sons were:
Leibish, Kopel, Mendel, Yossele, and Yehoshua.

Grandfather was Yossele Wohlberg, who married Roize;
they had six sons and three daughters;
their sons were:
Boruch, Asher, Yehoshuo Beirach, Kopel, Yirmiyohu, and Avrohom Yitzchok.

Father was Yirmiyohu, who married Hermina;
they had three sons and one daughter;
these were:
Yitzchok Zvi (Harry), Blanka (Blanche), Miklos (Max), and Yosef (Joseph);
Hermina later married Marcus Cohen,
and they had one daughter, Madeline.

Max married Theresa, and they had one son, Jeffrey;
Max later married Miriam and then Rochelle.
Jeffrey married Judy, and they had two sons and one daughter;
these are:
Adam, Jeremy, and Rachel.

Jeremy married Julie-Anne; Adam married Shira, and they had a daughter, Tamar.

APPENDIX B
Beiti—Beit Tefillah
Max Wohlberg

Dr. Abraham Heschel's perceptive and incisive article "The Task of the Ḥazzan" in the winter 1958 issue of *Conservative Judaism* prompts me to add some further observations on public worship and on matters relating to it, from the viewpoint of a *ḥazzan*.

The Place

In regard to our synagogues, it seems to me, we are derelict in two directions. On the one hand, in our zeal to stress their all-inclusive nature, we minimize their essential function as houses of prayer; on the other hand, in erecting magnificent structures, we fail to realize that lavishly (at times, garishly) appointed and visually impressive auditoriums are not ipso facto conducive to prayer. We either neglect to emphasize the importance of prayer, or we fail to perceive its requirements.

If we conceive of prayer as the greatest spiritual adventure of man, we must consider the necessary elements and the appropriate milieu on which depends the optimum realization of that adventure. The vital ingredients are inner and external. Dependence on external (visual, audible, sensual) elements is in inverse ratio to command of inner (ethical, spiritual, devotional) factors. As unfortunately few of us are capable of concentration to a degree that would make us oblivious to our surroundings, we must make every effort to create conditions sympathetic to our purpose. The ornate design of an edifice may astound and excite, but instead of inducing us to contemplate the majesty of God, it may be more likely to cause us to admire the creativity of man. A house of prayer seems to call for unpretentious dignity. While we may shy away from a literal translation of *ya'a aniyuta leyisra'el* [poverty agrees with Israel], an ostentatious display of wealth or art is surely not in true Jewish spirit. *Ve'asu li mikdash veshakhanti betokham* [and let them make Me a sanctuary, that I may dwell among them][1] seems to imply a sanctuary where both God and man may feel at home. A mood of humility and devotion is more likely in an atmosphere of mellow warmth than in one of complex artificiality. No structural adornment should divert the attention of the worshiper from his lofty purpose. While Israel directs his attention heavenward, he perseveres.[2]

The Atmosphere

Similarly, since unobstructed vision is currently the paramount desideratum, distracting activities should be eliminated. All necessary arrangements, including the distribution of honors, should be made with quiet, unobtrusive dispatch. A spirit of unconstrained orderliness should prevail. It is well to remember that those on the pulpit are there not to supervise and to direct the activities of the congregants, but rather to serve as exemplars in conduct and devotion. They are there not to see, but to be seen and to be emulated. *Einei amekha bam teluyot ve'eineihem lekha meyahalot* [the eyes of Your people are lifted up to them, and their eyes are lifted up to You].[3]

The *Siddur*

For approximately two thousand years, the *siddur* reflected the joy and the grief, the piety and the longing of our people. Its phrases mirrored the meditations of our hearts, and its spirit molded the length of our days. The words of the *Shema Koleinu* [hear our voices] were appropriate in every contingency, and the petition *Velamalshinim* [and for slanderers] was found suitable in every tragic era. Containing eternal verities, the *siddur* encompassed all that was temporary.

Although in dispersion, variations developed, the *siddur*'s underlying uniformity strengthened our peoplehood. Its expressions became constituent elements of our culture. To tamper with these in order to conciliate a contemporary concept is to do violence to the veritable and to the constant, for the sake of the variable and the current. To deny the aspirations of our an-

---

[1] Exod. 25:8.
[2] *Rosh Hashanah* 3:8.
[3] From the prayer *Heyei im pifiyot*.

cestors merely because our own would assume a different form or would be expressed in another manner is to slight our past and, by implication, impair the present.

Surely our exegetical propensities can be trusted to cope with any text in need of reinterpretation. As a matter of fact, archaic expressions and outmoded phraseology never prevented the faithful from praying. Language is in a constant process of evolution. New translations may indeed be needed for each generation, but to subject our time-hallowed prayers to the vagaries of vogue and to fleeting fashion seems to be callous and precipitous. There exists ample opportunity for our gifted men to contribute creatively in the province of prayer without doing damage to words sanctified during centuries of use. Let them give expression to our horrible decimation in modern *piyyutim* [poems], find words for our joy in Israel, and arouse our people from apathy and ignorance.

The Congregation

With facility in its language and affinity to the spirit of prayer, our predecessors developed a remarkable community of devotees. Though united in worship, each person uttered the same text, at his own pace, with his own inflection, invested with his own intent. The congregation consisted of united units. Enveloped by the *tallit* [prayer shawl], one had no need to see one's co-worshipers; the binding sounds of fervor spoke of common purpose, affirming their oneness. A soaring polyphony of inspired supplication reverberated through the charged atmosphere.

Today, in too many of our synagogues, co-attendants are seen, but no pious sound escapes their lips. Instead of a vibrant, assertive congregation, we behold a stolid and docile assemblage submissively complying with the directives of a vicar. No better proof need be cited in illustration of our cultural decadence than the tragic fact that the ability to read Hebrew, which three generations ago was a commonly acquired discipline, has in our own day become a rare mark of distinction. Congregational participation in the Hebrew is limited to a few threadbare tunes. Personal prayers have vanished. A blasé, gum-chewing, complacent audience, gingerly stifling a yawn, awaits to be entertained. *Ein omer ve'ein devarim beli nishma kolam* [unless one is audible, he has not said anything]. One lacking the magnanimity of R. Levi Yitzhok of Berditchev has difficulty in intoning the phrase *lekhol kehala kadisha hadein* [for this entire holy community]. Apathy, passivity, and reticence replaced fervor, passion, and commitment. The propitious time of a congregation in prayer, *eit ratzon besha'a shehatzibur mitpalelin*,[4] never materializes. Nor is His nearness sensed by those who call Him not in truth. The meaning of *kol atzmotai tomarna adonai* [all my bones declare the Lord] is beyond the ken of one ensconced in repose, as the intent of *salaḥti kidvarekha* [I have pardoned them, as you have asked] escapes the silent auditor.

Duration

The length of the service was debated almost since the inception of the synagogue service itself. R. Akiba,[5] R. Yoḥanan,[6] R. Meir,[7] and Samuel[8] favored brief supplications. While it was suggested[9] that time and circumstance may be determinant factors in deciding on the duration of prayers, the generally accepted premise is *eḥad hamarbeh ve'eḥad hamam'it uvilvad sheyekhavein libo lashamayim* [it makes no difference whether one lengthens or shortens his prayers as long as he directs his heart to heaven].[10] Prolonging a service beyond the ability of the worshipers to follow it with concentration and devotion is of doubtful value. On the other hand, a certain minimum time is required in preparation for public worship, sufficient to rid oneself of mundane and trite influences and to prepare for the sacred converse and awesome adventure. This need was provided for by the early Hassidim. *Ḥasidim harishonim hayu shohim sha'a aḥat umitpalelim kedei sheyekhavenu libam lamakom* [the early Hassidim were accustomed to wait one hour before praying in order to direct their hearts to God].[11]

Language

In setting the limits, as well as in planning the content of a service, we must, perforce, be mindful of the number who are fluent in the required languages. If we wish to retain Hebrew as the primary medium of our prayers, we must, of necessity, greatly increase our efforts to equip our congregants with the

---

[4] *Berakhot* 8a.
[5] Ibid., 31a.
[6] Ibid.
[7] Ibid., 61a.
[8] Ibid., 89a.
[9] Ibid., 34a.
[10] Ibid., 5b.
[11] Ibid., 34a.

ability to read Hebrew. A worthy desire to teach the grammar of, and conversation in, the languages need not be a concomitant of this effort.

We live in the shadow of a physically attractive and stimulating civilization, many of whose tenets and doctrines are antithetical and diametrically opposed to ours. A preponderant proportion of our people, except for an occasional contact with some "quaint" Jewish practice, find complete emotional fulfillment in the mores of that civilization. Customs fashioned by our forefathers, formed in the crucible of centuries and endowed with overtones of sublimity, are swallowed up by others of alien origin and foreign spirit, and the existence of the former is presently forgotten.

Those to whom our past is precious and those who crave the continuity of our tradition must preserve the unique nature of our worship and its language. The bulk of the traditional service could be retained even in congregations where only a minority are able to follow the Hebrew liturgy. Where this is not feasible, the salient elements of the service, in the order of its subdivisions, should be adhered to, with the eliminated passages divided for alternate weeks or for a five-week cycle. It is suggested that, as far as possible, the service continue on consecutive pages.

To deprive the doughty *daveners* of their devotions by diminishing the Hebrew elements in order to attract the neophytes is to give up a *bari* [certain] for a *shema* [doubtful] and to dehydrate the essential ingredients of a proven, life-enriching product. Salvation, it seems to me, lies in the other direction: in investing the traditional service with intensity and with *kavanah* [intention]. Such a service of heart and mind would serve as an irresistible attraction and as a potent incentive for the acquisition of the required facilities.

Kavanah

Even when granted an atmosphere of undisturbed tranquillity, a mood of devotion, a state of comprehension, and a facility of expression, the equality of *kavanah* may still be lacking. Those in search of it must learn that *kavanah* cannot be achieved piecemeal or in spurts.

Our attention must be whole, our intent complete. Our total being must be involved in this leap of faith. While it is possible to elevate parts of one's body in interrupted stages, the leap of a whole body can brook no arrest, can tolerate no *hafsaka* [interruption]. Distractions, even the most well intentioned, as long as they do not aid concentration in prayer, must be avoided.

The spirit aspiring to heavenly spheres must first overcome and resist all earthly gravitation. A mundane word, deed, or attitude may break its spell. *Ein omedin lehitpalel . . . ela mitokh divrei tora she'ein ba iyun* [i.e., study an uncomplicated matter of Torah before one stands to pray].[12]

During a service, I respectfully suggest, every word uttered should promote piety and abstain from producing agitation. Every sermon should aim to increase dedication. Although dissemination of Torah outweighs all other *mitzvot,* even it should not preempt the time of the service. *Mi shehaya osek batora vehigia zeman lehitpalel posek umitpalel* [if one is engaged in Torah study and the hour for reciting the *Amidah* arrives, one must break from his studies and pray].[13]

An aloof, clinical, dispassionate, analytical rationalization of matters of religious belief are deterrents to devotion. In the pulpit, Driver and Pfeiffer are no fit substitutes for *humash* with Rashi; Maritain is no proper replacement for the *Hafetz Hayyim* [book by R. Israel Mayer Kagen about gossip and slander]; Mead and Frazer belong in the classroom or lecture hall; and of what relation is Kierkegaard to Mount Sinai?

Inspiration and dissection are not properly consonant pursuits. Admiring a beautiful painting, one does not normally stop to consider the origin of the canvas. Nor is one, under the spell of an inspiring symphony, likely to ponder on the peculiarities of the English horn. Pity the singer during whose performance his listeners reflect on the function of his epiglottis!

The Cantor

Inherent in the nature of his calling—the blending of art with a religious function—is the cantor's addiction to a disease of disturbing dichotomy. This predisposition was intensified after the Renaissance by the upsurge of the Ars Nova and conditioned by the fact that the cantor was for centuries our people's sole exponent of the vocal art. The *ba'al tefillah* [master of liturgy] and the singer, the *hazzan* and the performer, the *sheliah tzibbur* and the artist vie with each other for supremacy. In the resolution of this conflict lies the measure of the man.

A study of ancient sources clearly reveals that if *hazzanut* is a *melekhet*

---

[12] *Mishneh Torah, Tefillah* 4:58.
[13] Ibid., 6:8.

hakodesh [holy task], the adjective is more compelling than the noun.[14] The esteem in which the precentor was held—the cantor stands like a cloaked angel of God,[15] *hakadosh barukh hu kishliah tzibbur* [God is like the prayer leader],[16] the special toasts in his honor—was not due to vocal prowess and musical attributes, but to his dedication to a sacred task. A lily among thorns, *keshoshana bein hahohim*[17] was the appropriate appellation of one able to lead his brothers in prayers. When, however, he was found wanting in desirable attributes, the reproving words of Jeremiah, "She hath uttered her voice against me; therefore I hated her," were applied to him.[18]

The required qualifications of a *hazzan* lie in diverse areas, such as attitude to God, relation to his people, liturgy, *nusah*, music, and voice. Foremost must be his love of God, which expresses itself in a strong desire to pray, complete absorption in the prayers, humility and piety that preclude pretense. It should be self-evident that one who dedicates his voice to the service of God ought not to use that voice to sing of carnal lust, of the vile and the vulgar. To be both a *hazzan* and an actor is like being both hot and cold, tall and short, black and white. One deals with truth and devotion, the other with pretense and deception. The use of *kelei kodesh* [Jewish clergy] ought to be restricted to their proper function. To sing *kadesheinu bemitzvotekha* [sanctify us through your commandments] on Friday evening and *La Traviata* the following afternoon is a travesty of aesthetics and a violation of religious sensitivity. It is, in essence, an equation of the two, the prayer and the play, on the level of a performance. Let us keep in mind that while man occupies center stage, God is featured on the pulpit. In the service of God, a vessel, though it burns, will not be consumed. Expose it to the searing flame of *eish zara*, a strange fire, and tragedy is inevitable.

Every moment of his life, the *hazzan* must remember that soon he is to be the spokesman of his congregation, that soon he is to address the Creator of the world. His is not an occasional role to be played in public, but a yoke of the Kingdom of Heaven that one cannot don and doff at will. His

---

[14]*Hullin* 24b; *Ta'anit* 16a; *Mishneh Torah, Tefillah* 8:11.
[15]*Midrash Tehillim* 17:5.
[16]*Rosh Hashanah* 17b.
[17]*Shir Hashirim Rabba* 2:7.
[18]Jer. 12:8.

ministry is continuous and is not limited to praying aloud on the pulpit. Yosele Rosenblatt, when asked by the chairman of a ritual committee why his fee for conducting services was higher than that of Mordechai Hershman, replied: *Ikh daven oikh di shtile shimenesrey* [I also pray the silent *Amidah* for you].

The cantor is a *sheliah tzibbur* when his outlook is colored by the history of his people and his intellect is affected by its literature; when he is sensitive to the sorrows and joys of the most modest of his congregants; when his personal life reflects the moral and religious precepts of his people and when in its customs is his delight; when his nation's tragedy is reflected in his voice and its hopes are echoed in his song. He must be a true *oheiv amo yisra'el* [one who loves his people Israel].

As *ba'al tefillah*, he should have as his domain the *dinei uminhagei beit hakeneset* [laws and customs of the synagogue], the *zemirot, selihot* [petitionary prayers], *kinot* [poems of lament], *mahzor, siddur,* their history and usage. A deep reverence for these sacred texts and a ready identification with their exalted sentiments are to be expected of him. He must indeed be a *yoreid lifnei hateiva* [one who descends before the Ark (to act as the prayer leader)], in both meanings of the last word in the Hebrew phrase, i.e., subservient to the word. *Yerida zo aliya hi* [this descent is an ascent]. He must be endowed with the faculty to sound each word, each phrase, as if uttered for the first time. He must each day find new inspiration in them in order to inspire others anew each day. Not content with superficial, *peirush hamilot* [literal translation of the words], he must seek the deeper, implied meaning of each word; text plus context, content plus connotation.

Nusah

Jewish ingenuity is clearly evident in the ability to discover myriads of unsuspected ideas and an endless variety of interpretations in the seemingly most simple statement. It is also significant to note that interpretations did not supersede one another but were utilized each at its opportune time. Variations in prayer texts, such as *nekadeish* and *na'aritzekha; emet veyatziv* and *emet ve'emuna; ahava rabba* and *ahavat olam,* were likewise retained and assigned to different services in order to add distinction to each of them. Even so, the melodies of the *te'amim* [tropal signs], each of which represents a definite musical theme, were changed in order to give special significance to the

Haftarah [prophetic readings], to the *Megillot*, and to the readings for the High Holy Days. Similarly, texts appearing in more than one service were often supplied with diverse tunes to give uniqueness to each service. Thus, the *Kaddish* may be chanted in three different modes on the weekdays. Three distinct *Kaddish* tunes are available for the festivals, four for the Sabbath, even for the High Holy Days. Special, so-called *misinai* [melodies that were given by God at Mount Sinai] were applied to a number of texts, and finally, set prayer modes were designated for specific sections of the liturgy. All this represents *nusaḥ*.

Strict adherence to it adds interest, color, beauty, and authenticity to the service. Solomon Geiger describes in meticulous detail the rigidly observed *nusaḥ* of Frankfurt am Main.[19] Referring to the Rosh Hashanah eve service, coincident with the Sabbath, he writes:

> The cantor sings the words *barekhu et Adonai* in the normal tune for Sabbath evening. However, when the cantor reaches the word *hamevorakh*, he uses the special High Holy Day tune for the evening service. The cantor should pray the evening service as if it were a normal Sabbath evening. The cantor should sing the end of the *keriat shema* and the interruptions in the prayer "true and firm" in the High Holy Day melody. The shofar is blown using the known melody. The *ḥatzi kaddish* is sung in the same tune in which the cantor sang the word *hamevorakh*. In every *Kaddish* that is sung, partially or entirely, in the special High Holy Day melody or in a melody chosen for the High Holy Days, one should add the word *ule'eila* to the prayer. However, those that sing the *Kaddish* with another known tune should not add *ule'eila* here in Frankfurt . . . and the *Kiddush* for the New Year is sung using the festival melody.[20]

To omit a traditional tune is to diminish our cultural heritage; to replace it with one that is new is an act of arrogance and conceit.

Music

Not content with a routine performance of *mitzvot*, our sages emphasized the need for *hidur mitzva* [beautification of the commandment]. What better way to guard against monotonous routine than with inspiring music? Text and

---
[19]*Divrei Kehillot* (Frankfurt am Main, 1862).
[20]Ibid., p. 131.

music thus became synonymous. In place of song, there will be prayer. The Levites spoke in song.[21] R. Meir attributed to song a quality of indispensability. The song is indispensable to the sacrifice.[22] Even the study of the Bible and the Mishnah was to be done with song.[23] Song was symbolic of all that was good.[24] What is meant by serving God with joy and gladness of the heart? The answer: song.[25]

It is the cantor's obligation to master the art of music and to employ it in the beautification of our ritual and in the enhancement of its musical elements. He is also required to improvise in a pleasant voice and in a stirring manner, within the designated prayer modes, and, if gifted, to compose in a style that will move the worshipers toward greater piety and deeper devotion. It would seem altogether worthwhile to remember that the purpose of synagogue attendance is the worship of God. The congregation, led by the *hazzan,* worships according to a formula that we call liturgy. Synagogue music is to interpret the liturgy. The means of art are to further this end; the greater the artist, the less obtrusive his art. A ceaseless effort toward greater congregational participation should be maintained, never permitting the metamorphosis of worshipers into an audience.

It is the *hazzan*'s duty to set high musical standards for the synagogue. He should endeavor to obviate the trite waltz tunes utilized for the glorious *Shema* and save the majestic *Adon Olam* from the vulgar rock 'n' roll treatment. He should resist noxious, albeit well-meaning, requests of popular tunes into the service. He must inform and teach the elusive subjects of good taste and propriety. *Im ein da'at havdala minayin* [without knowledge, how can one make a distinction?]. The "Anniversary Waltz," he must point out, is out of place in the synagogue, and not every jolly folk tune is necessarily appropriate for *Eil Adon* [the Lord Master]. In an otherwise admirable desire to bring life and vitality into the service, the theater and vaudeville stage have been combed for rollicking and hilarious tunes, forgetting that *lo harei ze ka-harei ze* [this case is different from the other], what fits here is likely to be a misfit elsewhere.

---

[21] *Berakhot* 6a; *Bikkurim* 3:4.
[22] *Arakhin* 11a.
[23] *Megilla* 32a.
[24] *Sifrei Deuteronomy* 26.
[25] *Arakhin* 10a.

It was, I believe, the Maggid of Mezeritch who noted that *besimḥa* [with gladness] and *maḥshava* [thought] consist of the same letters. Even in a state of rejoicing, we must be aware of taste and propriety. In cases of doubt, when faced with tunes of questionable quality, it is well to remember that intent and manner have the power to infuse sanctity into the mundane. Thus, a *niggun* [tune] finds its *tikkun* [remedy]. Thus can the God-intoxicated man attain physical abandon, spiritual cleansing, and fervent expression in the humblest of tunes. When, however, nobility of sentiment and religious fervor are absent, there remains only a hollow, pulsating, boisterous beat, a stamping of feet, in which head and heart have no part.

In our considerations of the nature of synagogue music, recognition of fundamental differences in the concept of music in church and in synagogue is essential. In the church, music of a cultivated caliber impresses itself upon the congregation and renders it receptive to an inspiring message. In the synagogue, the function of music is to enthuse and to ignite the worshipers spiritually, to raise them aloft, urging them on to find self- and soul-expression in seeking personal communion with the Almighty. In the church, the direction of music is downward; in the synagogue, upward. In the church, the music does something *to* the congregation; in the synagogue, it must do something *with* the congregation. In the church, its aim is impression and acquiescence; in the synagogue, it is expression and activity.

Because of various circumstances, synagogue music has not kept pace with the development of general music. Except for the works of a handful of composers who succeeded in merging a new technique with an old folk art, *nusaḥ* remained an aggregation of hundreds of melodic motifs, augmented by the incursion of new, often altered, tunes that were arranged, combined, and embellished by the cantor in conformity with his knowledge, temperament, and talent. While it is true that a number of uniquely gifted *ḥazzanim* succeeded in imbuing their art with a distinct hue and flavor, nevertheless its general genre remained in the folk province. The commonly employed motifs, many of them utilized for study and cantillation, were familiar to the congregation, who would often anticipate their sequence, development, and resolution. Thus, the cantor merely added color, ornament, and intensity to a musical concept present in the consciousness of the congregation.

The Composer

As matter in the hands of the master, to be done with in accordance with his will, was the *ḥazzanic* recitative. Condensed, expanded, adorned, molded, hummed, and exclaimed—yet its salient ingredients were clearly recognized or instinctively felt. Cantor and congregation also shared common knowledge in the implied and subtle meanings of numerous phrases of the liturgy. Tacit agreement existed as to the proper mood for certain passages and sections of the prayer book.

Herein lies the explanation as to why many composers writing for the synagogue fail to strike a responsive chord in congregants. Their failure must be ascribed to their ignorance of the intrinsic historical, cultural, and emotional intricacies of synagogue tradition. These composers, some highly talented, others merely facile technicians of music, may approach their task with laudable intentions, but alas, they lack genuine orientation. No serious thought need be given to the glib technician to whom the liturgy is merely a source of texts to be supplied with music. Most of their product is an aberration.

Of far greater interest is the effort of the serious musician who tries to convey the sentiments and emotions that a particular prayer or service arouses in him. This is, at times, profound music. In the absence, however, of traditional atmospheric, conceptual, and musical considerations, it fails to effect a bond with, or evoke an echo in, the worshiper, and thus can secure for itself no permanent place in the repertoire of the liturgy. Many manage to do something worthwhile *for* the worshiper. Some do something worthwhile *to* the worshiper, but few do anything worthwhile *with* the worshiper. Hence, since the criteria of *ḥazzan* and composer are not the same, they frequently do not see eye to eye. The former's frame of reference is custom and tradition, spirit and mood, *nusaḥ* and mode; his aim is to mold the old. The composer considers form and structure, technique and development; his goal is *veyashan mipenei ḥadash totzi'u*,[20] to replace the old. Obviously, the ultimate reconciliation of these divergent attitudes would bring about a blessed era of musical creativity and a revitalization of the liturgy. If faced with a choice between a musically anemic setting of a service that is nonetheless traditional in spirit, and one that is musically well conceived and technically well executed

---

[20] Lev. 26:10.

but lacking a fulcrum of tradition, I must risk the label of reactionary and prefer the former.

Lest I be accused of propagating the perpetuation of musical paucity and sterility and of callously condemning all current creativity, permit me to assert that I envisage a colossal task for the authentically prepared Jewish composer and long for his product. Majestic portions of our liturgy await adequate musical settings. Spurious and frivolous tunes need to be replaced with others of stirring dignity. Musically well balanced services, with due regard for cantor, congregation, and choir (often amateur) are sorely needed. These immense undertakings, however, should be conditioned on cognizance of and adherence to *nusah* and synagogue tradition and on patience to introduce changes gradually. With some hesitancy, I would nevertheless propose the formation of a National Synagogue Music Committee to pass on all new music introduced into the synagogue. A similar procedure has been established by the Church. Such a committee could also approve a *minhag amerika* [American rite] in cantillation. Myopia and astigmatism being prevalent afflictions, it is not wise to permit every man to do what is right in his own eyes.

Summary

Our liturgy is an immeasurably rich repository of heavenly inspired texts. Ethical instruction and spiritual insight fill its pages. Its reverent perusal will comfort and strengthen. Its dilution will impair and weaken. To transform each service into a profound experience is a challenge that promises most noble rewards. If we recognize that in the acceptance of this challenge, the *hazzan* occupies a prominent position, and if we admit that a tall *yarmulke* does not a *hazzan* make, it follows that the education of the *hazzan* cannot be suffered to become a peripheral, hit-or-miss affair. His multifaceted training cannot be doled out *kile'ahar yad* [casually], on a marginal basis.

In setting standards for the cantorate, we would do well to heed the advice of Maimonides: "Only the person greatest in wisdom and in deeds should be appointed to be the prayer leader"[27] and give ear to the opinion of the *Shulhan Arukh:* "His words and his melodies must always be pure and not inappropriate to the sanctity of God, and the same is true of the *hazzan*'s way

---

[27]*Mishneh Torah, Tefillah* 8:11.

of life."[28] It is needless to add that the elevation of the status of the cantorate cannot be achieved without the active help of our rabbis.

It is not in the power of the prisoner to release himself from prison.[29] In our efforts to add the ingredients of fervor, intensity, and dignity to the service, music has much to contribute. It may even succeed where other means may fail.

An attractive tale is told[30] of the "Tanya" (R. Shne'or Zalman), who, after a novel and poetic interpretation of the phrase *vekhol ba'alei hashir yotze'in beshir venimshakhin beshir* [masters of song exit and are led by song],[31] was asked to explain a number of difficult biblical passages. Instead of addressing himself to the questions, he began to sing with ardor and rapture. Suddenly, his interrogators, absorbed in thought and transported in ecstasy, perceived that all their questions had been answered, their doubts had disappeared, and all was right.

---

[28] *Oraḥ Ḥayyim* 57:581.
[29] *Berakhot* 5b.
[30] *Sipurei Ḥasidim* (Tel Aviv, 1954–55), 444.
[31] *Shabbat* 5a.

APPENDIX C
Shiru Lo
Max Wohlberg

Jewish liturgy has two salient qualities: it is congregation-oriented, and it has to be chanted in an agreeable manner. Although in the absence of an alternative, one is permitted to pray privately, synagogue attendance and participation in communal worship are mandatory. Indeed, we are warned not even to dwell in a place that is without a synagogue.[1] Furthermore, we are exhorted that a community without regular worship arouses the ire of the Almighty.[2]

The Talmud records a revealing dialogue between Rabbi Isaac and Rabbi Naḥman. Why, asked the former, does the master not attend synagogue prayer? I cannot, the latter replied. Then, continued Rabbi Isaac, why not collect a *minyan* at home? That, maintained Rabbi Naḥman, would involve me in too much trouble. Then, persisted Rabbi Isaac, why not ask the *ḥazzan* to inform you of the exact time of the congregational service so that you may synchronize your prayers with theirs? But look, asked Rabbi Naḥman, why all this fuss? Because, replied Rabbi Isaac, Rabbi Yoḥanan quoted Rabbi Simon ben Yoḥai (on Ps. 69:14, "But as for me, let my prayer be unto Thee, O Lord, in an acceptable time") as teaching: What time may be considered acceptable? When a congregation is at prayer.[3]

Frequent references to public worship are found in our early history. At the dedication of the First Temple, the very inception of our formal public worship, King Solomon prayed that the Lord "may hearken to the supplication of thy servant, and of thy people Israel."[4] He thus visualized the Temple

---
[1] *Sanhedrin* 17b.
[2] *Berakhot* 6b.
[3] Ibid., 7b.
[4] 1 Kings 8:30.

as a place appropriate for both personal and group prayer. It is also significant that many sections of our liturgy, which had originally been in the domain of private devotion, have gradually entered the realm of group prayer.[5]

We are told that the prayer of a congregation has definite advantages over that of an individual, in that the former never remains unanswered.[6] It is therefore not surprising that for the formal recitation of a number of prominent liturgical passages, the presence of a *minyan* is obligatory.[7] It is an accepted rule that items of special sanctity require the presence of a minimum of ten.[8] As a matter of fact, it is suggested that even for prayers not requiring a quorum, at least three be present: one to read and two to respond.[9]

The Midrash enumerates the five possible manners of prayer. Foremost is the communal prayer in the synagogue. Then, in diminishing order of value, are those in the field, at home, on one's bed, and in thought.[10] If one prays in the synagogue, the *Shulḥan Arukh* advises him to adjust his prayers so that he can first join the congregation and only then attend to his private prayers.[11]

Responses

While the role of the congregation is thus emphasized, we must also bear in mind that the role of the individual worshiper is not a passive one. His active participation is vital—indeed, indispensable.[12] Prayer and its response, benediction, and its amen are an inseparable unit.[13] A number of responses, such as *barukh sheim kevod malkhuto* (probably the oldest),[14] *hallelujah, amen* (not employed in the sanctuary), and *berikh hu,* form an integral part of the liturgy.

Our ancestors knew of various forms of responses, phonal chants.[15] The *Mekhilta* quotes Rabbi Nehemiah:

> The holy spirit rested upon Israel, and they uttered the Song (of the sea) in the manner in which we recite the *Shema*. According to Rabbi Akiba, it was recited

---

[5]*Berakhot* 60b; Ismar Elbogen, *Der jüdische Gottesdienst* (Leipzig, 1913), 15, 87; Eliezer Levy, *Yesodot Hatefillah* (Tel Aviv, 1961), 106.
[6]*Devarim Rabba* 2:7.
[7]*Mishnah Megillah* 2:7.
[8]*Berakhot* 21b.
[9]*Midrash Tehillim* 113:3.
[10]Ibid., 4:9.
[11]*Oraḥ Ḥayyim, Hilkhot Tefillah* 109. See also Rashi and Tosafot on *Berakhot* 21b and Rashi on *Sukkah* 38b.
[12]Joseph Heinemann, *Hatefillah Bitekufat Hatana'im* (Jerusalem, 1964), 18.
[13]T. J. *Ta'anit* 3:11.
[14]Elbogen, 495.
[15]Ibid., 496. See also *Sukkah* 38b.

as is the *Hallel.* Rabbi Eliezer ben Taddai said: Moses would first begin with the opening words. The Israelites would then repeat them after him and finish the verse with him.[16]

In addition to responses, the Jewish worshiper is enjoined to recite each service almost in its entirety with the rest of the congregation. Such phrases as *ve'ameru khulam, umashmi'im yaḥad bekol, kulam ke'eḥad onim, yaḥad kulam kedusha yeshaleshu* precede significant passages and bespeak the ideal of prayer in unison.

Congregational Song

But our liturgy was not merely recited in a monotone; it was chanted *bin'imah*—pleasingly. It is remarkable how replete our ancient literature is with references extolling the importance of song. Not only prayers were sung, but the study of Bible and Mishnah had to be tuneful.[17] The tune, it was believed, would facilitate the memorization of the text studied.[18]

In the dedicatory prayer of Solomon,[19] the Temple is designated as the forum for song (*rinah*) and prayer (*tefillah*). The Talmud stresses the dependence of the one upon the other.[20] The Midrash interprets *rinah* as praise of the Lord and *tefillah* as prayer for the needs of man.[21]

A detailed description of the Temple service during the reign of Hezekiah relates: "And the singers sang, and the trumpeters sounded; all this continued until the burnt offering was finished."[22] Indeed, according to Rabbi Meir, the song had predominance over the offering.[23] In an effort to assert the primacy of song, the Talmud ascribes a biblical source to it.[24] Elsewhere, we learn of the minutiae of the service in the Second Temple and of the important role of music in its scheme.[25]

The one condition required of this song was that it be pleasant. God, we are assured, loves to hear a pleasant voice.[26] In a charming homily, the story is

---

[16] *Mekhilta Exod.* 15:1.
[17] *Megillah* 32.
[18] *Sanhedrin* 99b with Rashi.
[19] 1 Kings 8:28.
[20] *Berakhot* 6a.
[21] *Devarim Rabba* 2:1.
[22] 2 Chron. 29:28.
[23] *Arakhin* 11a.
[24] Ibid.
[25] *Mishnah Tamid* 7:3, 4; *Mishnah Bikkurim* 3:4; Rashi on *Kiddushin* 71a.
[26] *Midrash Tehillim* 33:1.

told of ten men who appeared before the heavenly throne and wished to sing a hymn to God. He said to them: "All of you are pleasing, pious, praiseworthy, and capable of singing before me. But I choose this one, because his voice is mellow."[27] We are also informed that although He will accept the tribute rendered by musical instruments, His preference is for vocal music.[28]

Rashi, who on occasion served as a *sheliaḥ tzibbur*, appreciated the favorable effects of fine singing. He comments on 1 Kings 8:28: "In the synagogue, the congregation recites songs and praises in a pleasant voice."[29] Discussing the qualifications of a preceptor on fast days, Rashi remarks that the sweetness of a voice captivates the heart.[30] It was thus inevitable that a pleasant voice became a prime requisite for a *ḥazzan*.[31]

The Tunes

Considering our ancestors' strong attachment to congregational singing, it may be surprising to note how few congregational tunes have been transmitted to contemporary worshipers. The following reasons may explain this anomaly.

1) The congregational song familiar in ancient times was, as it still is in most Eastern synagogues, a limited chant, a primitive form of *Sprechgesang*, frequently with a melismatic ending. The tunes sung today are of more recent origin and have not achieved the familiarity of the old.
2) Many congregational tunes were associated with holiday *piyyutim*. Not all these were employed by all rites (*minhagim*).
3) When a *piyyut* fell into disuse, its melody became obsolete.
4) *Ḥazzanim*, in an effort to be creative, sometimes replaced ancient tunes with compositions in "modern" style. (In Sephardic congregations, where the *ḥazzan* did not parallel the musical creativity of his Ashkenazic colleague, congregational singing flourishes.)
5) As a result of recurrent migrations and consequent exposure to new and different ethnic musical influences, old chants were altered, replaced, and forgotten.
6) New communities were often denied the services of competent *ḥazzanim* with knowledge and appreciation of the congregational chant.[32]

---

[27] *Shir Hashirim Rabba* 4:8.
[28] *Midrash Tehillim* 149:5.
[29] *Berakhot* 6a.
[30] *Ta'anit* 16a.
[31] *Mishneh Torah, Ahava, Hilkhot Tefillah* 8:11.
[32] B. Jacobson, *Der israelitische Gemeinde: Gesang* (Leipzig, 1884), 52.

7) Under the influence of "star" *ḥazzanim,* the bravura recitative gained emphasis, and the traditional chant and *nusaḥ* were neglected.
8) As the knowledge of Hebrew among our worshipers dwindled, and as the frequency of their attendance in synagogue decreased, so the role of the congregational song was reduced.
9) Frequently, the professional choir preempted the congregational melody.

Recent Attempts

The first serious attempt in modern times to involve the congregation musically took place in the early nineteenth century. The founders of the Reform movement, in their effort to emulate the Protestant church service, introduced hymns in the vernacular. A few of these, serving as preludes and postludes for the sermon and appropriate to the observance of national holidays, the Sabbath, weddings, and youth services, penetrated the so-called Moderate Reform congregations, particularly in Germany, Austria, and Hungary.

These congregations in the main followed the traditional liturgy but adopted moderate or external reforms. Decorum, formality, choir singing (mostly male), a sermon in the vernacular (although German was often utilized in Hungary as well as in the United States), and the elimination of the excesses of cantorial improvisation were the mark of these congregations. In essence, these were the prototypes of our contemporary Conservative congregations.

This marked the beginning of congregational participation in the music of the service. However, it must be noted that it was in the Conservative synagogue in the United States that congregational singing of the liturgy in Hebrew achieved its greatest popularity. There, as in no other place, it was welcomed, and there it flourished. For decades, it was a distinctive aspect of the Conservative synagogue. Gradually, this "Conservative" practice began to be adopted in Orthodox and Reform congregations, and except for a few dyed-in-the-wool, ultra-traditional Reform congregations, it is today a *sine qua non* in the American synagogue.

Literature

Unfortunately, few composers concerned themselves with congregational song. Solomon Sulzer's (1804–90) exclusive concerns were the purification and recording of the ancient *nusaḥ* and the creation of a choral repertoire for the entire calendar.[43] Of this enormous task, he acquitted himself nobly. He

---

[43]*Schir Zion* (Vienna, 1838–65).

created the model and supplied most of the elements of a well-organized musical service, but the element of congregational song is absent in his works.

This omission was noted and rectified by Louis Lewandowski (1821–94), who, in the foreword to his *Kol Rina Usefillah* (Berlin, 1871), bemoans the fact that congregations that previously shouted have been, since the introduction of choirs, condemned to silence. He also laments the fact that ungifted and unmusical individuals introduced trivial tunes into the service. In this work, Lewandowski provides abundant opportunities for the congregation to sing and many simple tunes for the purpose.

Of other works intended solely for congregational singing, at least three must be mentioned: *Gesänge für Synagogen* (Braunschweig, 1843) by H. Goldberg; *Schire Beth Jacob* (Altona, 1880) by L. Liebling and B. Jacobsohn; and the anonymous *Liturgisches Liederbuch* (Berlin, 1912).

In the United States, the melodies of Rabbi Israel Goldfarb, who taught *hazzanut* at the Jewish Theological Seminary, gained wide popularity. His settings for "Shalom Aleikhem," "Vayekhulu," "Magen Avot," and others have become staples in the synagogue repertoire. A. W. Binder and A. Z. Idelsohn contributed liberally to this branch of music. A. Goldenberg and this writer composed works—now outdated—for congregational singing. Legions of cantors and lay musicians have introduced original tunes or rearranged older ones.

Analysis

A survey of these tunes reveals such heterogeneous sources as Yiddish folk and theater song, dance tunes, pseudo-Oriental melodies, operatic and popular songs, Sephardic and Hassidic tunes, and, more recently, Israeli songs. At least two-thirds of them have the flavor of the shtetl.

The Hassidic tune, it should be noted, is in a category of its own. It is not subject to critical musical analysis. The qualities of pious fervor and ecstatic yearning that imbue its singers place it outside the realm of analytical consideration. To introduce it into a sedate and formal service is to commit an aesthetic blunder. Similarly, a pleasant *zemirot* tune is not necessarily appropriate for a liturgical text.

Irrespective of the melodic quality of the song, the desire of the average congregation to join in the singing is so great that it will without hesitancy appropriate the melody line of a choral composition. Thus, the choral music for the Torah service by Sulzer and Dunayevsky is sung today in unison by hundreds of congregations. As a matter of fact, the two are effortlessly intertwined. At Av Harahamim, the Sulzer setting is abandoned—not without logic—for the Dunayevsky music; and at Vay'hi Binesoa, a return is made to Sulzer.

The congregation's determination to sing will not be thwarted by the excessive range of a melody ("Hashiveinu") or by its chromatic alterations ("Hodo," Sulzer and Lewandowski). Alas, all too often the urge to sing, coupled with a lack of discernment, results in a congregation intoning the majestic "Adon Olam" to a tune better fitting the atmosphere of a beer hall. At times, a melancholy melody is attached to a text devoid of sad content, and at other times, the jolliest of tunes accompanies the description of an animal offering ("Uveyom Hashabbat").

The area of congregational singing is an expanding one. New texts are being suggested, requiring new and appropriate musical settings. One obvious source for these is our choral literature. To reduce a full-bodied choir selection to a congregational song requires musical sensitivity. However, the fact must be faced that in doing so, one not merely rearranges but transforms the music. What was before a complex edifice is now a simple house. True, the latter, in the hands of a competent craftsman, will receive the essential planning, execution, and polish. Nonetheless, it has undergone a metamorphosis, and to compare it with the original source would involve us in a venture of futility.

Furthermore, the musical ideas employed in a choral composition are not identical to or comparable with the ideas appropriate for a congregational tune. The latter requires an altogether different approach and demands unique technical considerations. While it is not feasible to discuss here in detail the melodic elements of congregational song, it is proper at least to point to general qualities legitimately expected of it. These would embrace congeniality with the text, consonance with the *nusah*, harmony with the mood of the service, conformity with the dignity of the synagogue, restriction to texts traditionally assigned to the congregation, limited vocal range, melodic ease, and rhythmic tractability.

Although the discriminating singer can, by the manner of his singing, avoid some of the objectionable qualities inherent in a trite tune, he should never introduce tunes of vulgar quality. While a joyful, rousing song in a suitable place ("Lekha Adonai Hagedullah," "Ein Keloheinu") is perfectly acceptable, we must beware of crossing the tenuously delineated border between joy and levity and between enthusiasm and frivolity. The conscientious composer, we should add, need not avoid originality, but in his search for useful melodic material, he could with profit examine *nusah,* cantillation motifs, Mi Sinai tunes, and Sephardic and Oriental Jewish melodies.

Two volumes, entitled *Zamru Lo,* published by the Cantors Assembly, contain an abundance of congregational tunes for the Friday evening and Sabbath morning services. However, the collection is rather more inclusive than selective. Thus, there are 14 melodies for "Adon Olam," 12 for "Yismah Moshe," 10 for "Av Harahamim," 15 for "Sim Shalom," 19 for "Lekha Dodi," and 18 for "Veshameru." In this case, the talmudic aphorism *kol hamosif gore'a* [to add is to detract] seems applicable. Nevertheless, these volumes can serve as the foundation for any serious study of the subject.

Texts

Careful thought should also be applied to the selection of meaningful and inspiring passages in the liturgy. There seems to be no justification for a lusty singing of "Uveyom Hashabbat" or "Atah Hu Shehiktiru" at the end of "Ein Keloheinu." The editors and publishers of new editions of prayer books and *mahzorim* could be of great help in indicating, by contrasting type or indentation, the appropriate passages for congregational singing. Such underscoring will prompt composers to supply the needed musical settings. Attention should also be given to the placement of these tunes in the service. It is wrong to crowd most congregational melodies into one section of the service and dole them out sparingly or withhold them entirely in other sections.

I will not dwell here on the technical aspect of accompaniment. I believe that the role of accompaniment is a subservient one. Its one task and sole justification is to be of help to the congregation. It is not to assume an independent role.

Today, a eulogy in praise of congregational singing is an anachronism. Two of the many services that I attended this past summer in Jerusalem were at Beth Hillel and in a Yemenite synagogue. Musically, the two had nothing in common, but the total, vocally spirited involvement present in both congregations was stirring beyond words.

The subject of worship in song and the problems inherent thereto would seem to merit the appointment of a permanent committee of composers, cantors, and rabbis. The findings and recommendations of so representative a committee would, I believe, be influential in raising the standards of a hitherto neglected area of Jewish life.

Having just returned from a visit to Israel, it seems to me that in regard to the music of our liturgy, ours is a crucial age calling for assiduous and meticulous labors. I view the enormous tasks awaiting urgent attention in three different stages and on three distinct levels: (1) To collect and to record the music of all formerly far-flung, now defunct, Jewish communities. This can be done while some of the she'erit hapleitah *is with us; (2) To cleanse and purify the collected material. This difficult task of study, analysis, research, and comparison requires knowledgeable and trained musicologists; (3) Gifted composers who, having absorbed the results of these efforts would endeavor to write a* nusah *for* klal Yisra'el, *combining the three main branches of Judaism: the Ashkenazim, the European Sephardim, and the Oriental Sephardim. There is now discernible throughout the Jewish world a conscious approach between the divergent factions of Jewry. I can think of no more effective method to strengthen the approach and to cement the ultimate fusion than through a common mode of worship. The need is present. Will the men equipped for this task respond?*

—Wohlberg, **Pirkei Hazzanut**, The Cantors Voice 13, no. 1
(September 1962)

APPENDIX D
Minutes of the Cantors Ministers Cultural Organization, 1938–40
Max Wohlberg

The fact of the matter was that progressively the cantors ceased to look to the Farband for the solutions to their problems. Thus, I was not surprised to receive the following frantic letter, dated October 28, 1938:

> Dear Colleague:
>
> We have just received information that the Jewish Council has engaged a prominent rabbi to place all refugee cantors in America. Therefore, we are calling this conference to find ways and means to solve our problems, as we are all in danger of losing our positions. Are you interested in protecting the cantorate? You know that in the last few years, our position has deteriorated more and more.
>
> The conference will be held on Monday, October 31, at 8 p.m. at the Community House, 270 West 89th Street, New York City. It is very urgent that you attend to protect yourself and the cantor profession.
>
> The Committee: P. Jassinowski, E. J. Kritchmar, A. Katchko, A. Friedman, D. Roitman, J. Schwartz

I have no recollection of the results of this conference. No doubt, during discussion in a calmer atmosphere, the threats disappeared and the positions were saved. I do, however, recall a number of telephone calls and a few informal, social get-togethers. Turning to my notebook, I read:

First Board Meeting

A meeting of the board of directors of the Chazzanim Ministers Alliance-K'neset Hachazzanim D'New York took place on December 7, 1938, at 12 noon, at Temple Ansche Chesed, West 100th Street in New York City. Glantz presided, and the following were present: Kwartin, Roitman, Friedman, Schwartz, Goldenberg, Hershman, Ringel, Katchko, B. Kwartin, Brodsky, Kritchmar, and Wohlberg. The first item on the agenda was the election of officers. The following were elected, all unanimously:

> Glantz, Hershman, and Katchko as members of a presidium
> Schwartz as treasurer
> Friedman as financial secretary
> Wohlberg as recording secretary
> Ringel as corresponding secretary

Subsequent to a motion made by Wohlberg, seconded by Roitman, an Examination and Acceptance Committee was appointed to pass on and to approve all candidates for membership in our organization. The committee is to consist of Goldenberg, Glantz, Hershman, Katchko, and Schwartz.

Upon motion made by B. Kwartin, seconded by Goldenberg, it was decided that all present members are subject to ratification by the examination committee. After a lengthy discussion, it was agreed to permit each member to decide for himself whether he wishes to belong to any other cantorial organization. Glantz is requested and agrees to submit a paper outlining a cultural, social, and ethical program for general discussion at our next meeting. The board, by majority vote, submits for approval the proposition that our dues be $8 per annum.

A Culture and Music Committee was appointed to prepare lectures, musicales, debates, and discussions, open to the lay public as well as to members. The Committee consists of Goldenberg, Katchko, Glantz, B. Kwartin, Schwartz, and Wohlberg.

Our next general meeting will take place on Wednesday, December 14, at Steinway Hall, New York City, when Glantz will read a paper on a subject relating to our profession. Meeting adjourned 3:20 p.m.

Max Wohlberg,

Recording Secretary

General Meeting, December 14, 1938, at Steinway Hall

Glantz presiding. Minutes of board of directors accepted. Motion made by Levitt, seconded by Erstling, to approve election of all officers. Examination and Acceptance Committee is ratified and augmented by addition of Ephros and B. Kwartin. It is decided that a majority (4) of this committee (of 7) is empowered to accept candidates subject to ratification by the board. Members objecting to any candidate are to voice their objections at a meeting of the board. Ephros is added to the Cultural Committee.

After a lengthy debate—in which the following participated: Schwartz, Erstling, Wohlberg, Friedman, Lange, Weisfeld, Katchko, Z. Kwartin, Brodsky, and Glantz—the body, by majority vote of two, reaffirms its previous decision not to interfere with any of our members who wish to continue their affiliation with other cantorial organizations. It is decided, by unanimous vote, that no officer of our organization is to accept office in another such organization, nor is his name to appear on its stationery. Annual dues of $8 ratified. After a short recess, the date for our next meeting is set for December 28, at which time the previously scheduled lecture by Glantz will be delivered. Meeting adjourned at 5 p.m.

Board of Directors Meeting, December 21, 1938, at Ansche Chesed

Present: Hershman, Ringel, Glantz, Lange, Friedman, Schwartz, Kwartin, Goldenberg, Roitman, Kritchmar, and Wohlberg. After a comprehensive discussion concerning the future of our organization, Glantz suggests that it be named "American Cantors Cultural Organization." Schwartz proposes "Chazzan Ministers Cultural Organization." By majority vote, the board decides to submit for approval the name of Cantors Ministers Cultural Organization. Glantz submits a minimum and a maximum program. The first (fraternal, social, and cultural) to be adopted at once; the latter to strive for and to pursue in the immediate future.

The first part consists of eight points:

1. Monthly musicales where new compositions of our members be performed, discussed, and analyzed.
2. Occasional forums, lectures, and discussions on the history of the cantorate (including biographies), covering both the Orthodox and the Reform factions of our profession.
3. Improvement of the ethical standards in our profession and the formation of an Arbitration Committee.
4. Refining the forums of publicity employed by our members.

5. Establishing a semiannual concourse for new liturgical compositions and sponsoring half-yearly chamber concerts for the performance of new compositions.
6. Endeavor to control and extend the musical education of our children in Talmud Torahs and to supervise the *nusha'ot* taught them.
7. Social and fraternal help for our colleagues in need.
8. Grant scholarship in advanced musical institutions for talented composers among our members.

The maximum program consists of five parts:

1. Group insurance.
2. A cantors' seminary for talented applicants.
3. Erection or purchase of a cantors' old-age home in Eretz Yisra'el.
4. Publication of a monthly bulletin.
5. Organization of a society to be known as "Friends of the Cantorate"—Chovevei Chazzanim BeAmerika.

Friedman would abolish the singing of prayers on the radio. Schwartz would immediately inaugurate the publication of a bulletin and the organization of an ensemble. Roitman opposes, Katchko favors a cantors' ensemble. Lange is in favor of sponsoring a radio program. Schwartz and Friedman are appointed to serve on a Finance Committee under the chairmanship of Z. Kwartin. It is decided that Hershman is to preside at our next general meeting until the scheduled lecture, when Katchko is to take over the chair.

General Cultural Meeting, December 28, 1938, at Steinway Hall

Hershman presiding. Minutes accepted. Schwartz greets Walter Davidson (for many years, president of Reform cantors), Kahn (from Liverpool), P. Jassinowski, and all assembled. Chairman introduces Miss Weiss, cellist, and Dr. Yokel, her accompanist, who render a short musical program consisting of works by Mendelssohn, Kodaly, and Mozart. Chairman thanks artists and introduces Glantz, who delivers a scholarly and instructive discourse, "The Definition of the Cantorate." A discussion follows, with Katchko presiding, in which the following participate: Wohlberg, Roitman, Oppenheim, Schwartz, Jassinowski, Goldenberg, Brodsky, Kwartin, Steinberg, Katchko, and Ephros. The last proposes an evening devoted to the memory of Idelsohn. Glantz gives a thorough résumé of all questions and comments. Kahn, who recently arrived in this country, graciously consents to sing a selection.

Board of Directors Meeting, January 4, 1939, at Ansche Chesed

Glantz presiding. Minutes accepted. Wohlberg moves a letter of appreciation be sent to Glantz for his recent lecture. Katchko moves that similar letter be sent to Miss Weiss and Dr. Yokel. After lengthy discussion, it is decided, on motion by Wohlberg, that at every board meeting we select a chairman and a substitute to serve at the next general meeting. Wohlberg is appointed to inform the press of all our activities. It is decided that we acquire permanent headquarters. It is also decided that at our next general meeting (January 11), Schwartz is to preside with Wohlberg as substitute. Meeting will be followed by continued discussion on the subject presented by Glantz. Cultural Committee meeting is to be called for one hour preceding the general meeting.

General Meeting, January 11, 1939, at Pythian Center, 135 West 70th Street

Schwartz presiding. Chairman urges all to come punctually to meetings. Minutes accepted. Motion made by Ephros to arrange a memorial meeting in honor of the late scholar Professor A. Z. Idelsohn is accepted.

Program submitted by Wohlberg. Schwartz, Katchko, Friedman, Ephros, Lange, Kwartin, Oppenheim, Rosowsky, Hyman, Vigoda, and Glantz discuss program. Katchko moves that Cultural Committee should make all arrangements for the memorial meeting. Wohlberg moves to table motion for engaging the Pythian Center as our permanent headquarters. Ten minutes recess.

Chairman welcomes Mr. J. Dymont, who describes tragic plight of the cantors in Berlin. William Sauler, accompanied by Dymont, sings one of the latter's (secular) compositions and is then thanked by the chairman. Kwartin, Putterman, and Schwartz discuss program of Glantz.

(Note: William Sauler, our recently departed colleague, was a gentle soul and a fine singer. He was also the student [in Berlin] of J. Dymont, the gifted composer of Rinat Ya'akov, a Sabbath eve service [including Minchah] for cantor, mixed choir, and organ. It was this writer's privilege to have Dymont conduct his High Holy Day choir at the Inwood Hebrew Congregation.)

CANTORS MINISTERS CULTURAL ORGANIZATION
MEMORIAL MEETING

Tendered in Honor of
Abraham Z. Idelsohn
Wednesday, January 25, 1939
Eight p.m. Sharp
at
The Society for the Advancement of Judaism
15 West 86th Street, New York City

PROGRAM

1.	Introductory Remarks	Adolph Katchko
2.	Opening Address	Leib Glantz, Chairman
3.	Psalm 1	Zeidel Rovner
4.	The Personality of Idelsohn	Gershon Ephros
5.	"Enosh Kechozir," by L. Lewandowski	Sung by choir under the direction of Zavel Zilberts
6.	Representative Works of Idelsohn	Max Wohlberg
7.	"Hayad'u Hal'vavoth" (Halévy-Idelsohn) Quartet	with Z. Zilberts
8.	Idelsohn as Musicologist	Jacob Beimel
9.	"Habeit Mishomayim" (Zilberts)	Choir of Z. Zilberts
10.	"Eil Molei Rachamim"	Zavel Kwartin
11.	Closing Remarks	Chairman

Meeting of the Board of Directors, February 1, 1939, at Steinway Hall

Glantz presiding. Minutes accepted. Report of memorial meeting given by Friedman, Erstling, and Wohlberg. It is decided to thank all who helped make it a moral success. Hershman, Glantz, Friedman, Erstling, Katchko, Wohlberg, Lange, Kwartin, Steinberg, and Brodsky discuss the letter received by most of our members from the Cantors Association (*Hazzanim Farband*). It is decided unanimously to appoint a committee of three—Glantz, Kwartin, and Wohlberg—to present our views at the next meeting that the *Farband* may call, for the purpose of discussing the status of our organization. It is also decided unanimously that all our members sign a declaration of allegiance to our organization. The form of declaration is to be prepared by the above committee.

At our next meeting, Glantz will be chairman and Wohlberg his substitute. It is decided to inform Professor Weinberg that our organization has as yet not decided its position regarding sponsoring publications. The board decides that if one of its members does not attend two successive meetings, he is to receive a special letter from the board. If the letter remains unanswered, that member is automatically suspended from the board.

General Meeting, February 8, 1939, at Steinway Hall

Glantz presiding. Minutes accepted. Friedman and Schwartz report on the memorial meeting in memory of Professor Idelsohn. Letter was received from L. Saminsky stating his regrets at his inability to attend the memorial meeting. Glantz reports on the letters received by many of our members from the *Farband* and describes our meeting with them yesterday. He also submits their proposal that we continue our existence under their name. Hershman, Schwartz, Roitman, Wohlberg, Friedman, Lange, Saltzman, Meisels, Erstling, Katchko, Kwartin, and Jassinowski discuss this proposal.

Miss Cynthia Jassinowski is introduced and plays two very effective piano selections. Her father then recites two poems from his most interesting book, *Symphonische Gesangen*. Glantz expresses our regrets to M. Nathanson for having indirectly slighted him in our arrangement of the Idelsohn meeting in his congregation. Previous discussion is resumed. The proposal of the *Farband* is unanimously voted down. The question of a charter for our organization is referred to our board of directors. The chairman reads the Declaration of Allegiance, which is be signed by every member. It is accepted unanimously. Meeting adjourned.

Board of Directors Meeting, February 15, 1939, at Ansche Chesed

Glantz presides. Minutes accepted. Katchko proposes that we invite Mr. Jules Chajes as lecturer for our next cultural meeting on February 23, to which the general public will be invited. Proposal accepted. Wohlberg is to act as chairman. A raffle (for one dollar) of various liturgical books will then take place. Refreshments will be served, for which purpose Ringel donates the sum of $5. The balance of the needed sum will be supplied by the board. The charter and form of the Declaration of Allegiance is deferred for next meeting. Wohlberg reports on the meeting of the *Farband* where our answer to their proposal of amalgamation was discussed.

Cultural Meeting, February 23, 1939, at Ansche Chesed

Glantz presides, discusses the theme scheduled for the evening and introduces Mr. Jules Chajes, an accomplished musician and composer who gives a lecture, "Jewish Music: Past and Future." Appropriate musical selections are rendered by Miss Zina Alvers, soprano, and Miss Shulamit Silber, violinist, both accompanied by Mr. Chajes. A raffle of twelve cantorial books is conducted by Wohlberg, Rappaport, Mmes. Ringel and Erstling. $25.55 is realized. After a short discussion, refreshments are served by courtesy of Ringel and members of the board of directors.

Board of Directors Meeting, March 1, 1939

Glantz presides. Glickstein (of Boston) is present as guest. Problem of membership is discussed. The examination and acceptance committee will meet Monday at 1 p.m. to review the list of our membership. An application form, which will have to be filled out and signed by all applicants, will be submitted by Wohlberg and Ringel. At our next general meeting, "Ethical Problems of the Cantorate" will be the title of a lecture by Wohlberg. Bernard Kwartin will speak on "the voice." Official thanks are extended to Katchko for providing a meeting room for our sessions. Program for the following Cultural Meeting will be prepared by the presidium and the Culture Committee. Glantz proposes to use the services of a typist for our mailings.

General Meeting, March 8, 1939, at Steinway Hall

Glantz presides. Chairman introduces Miss Elsy Stein, violinist, Miss Valy Gara, cellist, and Miss Sophie Feuerman, pianist, who play a Beethoven trio. Wohlberg speaks on ethical problems of the cantorate. The guest artists play a Mendelssohn trio, after which there is a general discussion on the subject presented by Wohlberg. The following participate: Roitman, Vigoda, Beimel, Marvitt, Hershman, Brodsky, Erstling, and Glantz. Levitt asks our organization to help a fine Jew, convicted of a federal offense, by asking the sentencing judge for leniency.

(Note: I am copying the following report from a somewhat faded, penciled yellow sheet.)

Joint meeting of the Jewish Ministers Cantors Association (Hazzanim Farband) and the Cantors Ministers Cultural Organization on March 13, 1939, at the Farband locale at 111 Houston Street

Finestone (of Hebrew Trades Union), chairman. Glantz reiterates our position, stating that the Cultural Organization will function in cultural areas, leaving economic problems to the union. Kapov-Kagan accuses us of insincerity in our desire for culture. He suggests either a reorganization of the cantorate or our leaving the *Farband*, to form a completely new organization. Erstling declares our perfect right to meet with men of fine standing in the profession and not with those who are essentially outside of it. He also denounces the union. Breitman stresses that no school for cantors has as yet been established by those now preaching "culture," and our absence at meetings, rehearsals, and other functions proves that we have actually broken away. Lipitz agrees with Kapov-Kagan and claims that our purpose is merely to oppose the union. He emphasizes the impossibility of the existence of two cantorial organizations.

Yardeini takes the floor. Schwartz affirms the inability of the union to help the cantorate and bemoans our sufferance, in the midst, of men carrying two union books. He adds that two organizations can collaborate after reorganization. Maison says that all need culture, but bread takes precedence. Wohlberg points to the need for a place reserved for cultural pursuits. Hershman disclaims political interests and warns *Farband* that expelling us would ruin it. Walitzky states that listening to a lecture is not synonymous with the acquisition of culture.

Goldstone takes floor—then sits down. Finestone fears that our separate existence will ultimately lead to an open break and is of the opinion that we ought to educate all and not create an aristocracy. He proposes the selection of a smaller joint committee (three of each group) to discuss the issue. Glantz echoes the wish for duly appointed committees of both organizations.

Board of Directors Meeting on March 16, 1939, at Rappaport's Restaurant on Second Avenue

Glantz, chairman. Wohlberg reports on our meeting with *Farband*. Letter was received by Glantz from *Farband*, inviting our committee to meet with their committee at office of Gewerkschaften on Monday. Chairman wishes us to reaffirm our previous position. After lengthy discussion, it is decided to: 1) induce our members to continue affiliation with union; 2) retain, if possible, our present name; and 3) cooperate fully with the *Farband*. Representing us at the joint meeting will be Glantz, Hershman, and Katchko, with Schwartz and Wohlberg as substitutes.

Board of Directors Meeting, March 22, 1939, at 418 Central Park

Glantz (chairman) reports on meeting of our presidium with the *Farband* at Hebrew Trades Union. Proposal was made there by E. Spivack that our organization exist as a branch of the *Farband* with autonomy in its functions that should be open to all cantors. After prolonged discussion, no decision is reached.

Board of Directors, April 24, 1939, at 4800 14th Ave., Brooklyn, New York

Glantz, chairman. Letter received by Glantz from Finestone is read and is referred to next general meeting (April 27). Cultural meeting will take place on Wednesday, May 3. Program (improvisation) will be prepared by Glantz, Katchko, and Wohlberg. Ringel is officially thanked for acting as secretary in absence of Friedman. List of our members in arrears is read. It is decided to remind them of this lapse in our next mail. A most interesting discussion follows on the subject of modulation, after which Mrs. Hershman serves a delicious lunch.

Max Wohlberg

Business Meeting, April 27, 1939, at Steinway Hall

Glantz presiding. Chairman reports on our conferences with the *Farband* and reads the letter we received from M. Finestone, secretary of the Gewerkschaften, who acted as mediator between the two groups. Wohlberg reports on the last meeting of *Farband,* where autonomy in the selection of members was offered our organization upon its amalgamation with the *Farband.* Hershman, Friedman, Goldenberg, Roitman, Schwartz, Erstling, Kwartin, Katchko, Putterman, Lange, Ephros, Weisser, Weisfeld, Jassinowski, Steinberg, and Glantz discuss proposal. Upon motion by Wohlberg, seconded by Erstling, it is decided that: 1) although desiring to cooperate fully with the *Farband,* we cannot, for multiple reasons, become its branch; 2) we are unwilling to limit our membership to union men. Motion is carried unanimously.

Cultural Meeting, May 3, 1939, Steinway Hall

Glantz, chairman. Program: Beimel reads a paper on improvisation. Zeidel Rovner, Sholom Greenspan, and D. M. Steinberg improvise successive verses of "Av Horahamim." Glantz discusses problem of improvisation. Glazer, Roitman, Kritchmar, and Goldenberg sing parts of "Ato Nigleiso." Jassinowski gives his view on improvisation. Wohlberg, Hershman, Friedman, Roitman, A. W. Binder, Lange, and Rappaport discuss the subject in great detail.

Board of Directors Meeting, May 10, 1939, at Ansche Chesed

Wohlberg, chairman. Roitman and Glantz report on our last cultural meeting, at which one of our members (M. Hershman) expressed himself in a manner unbecoming the dignity of our profession and the decorum of our sessions. After condemnations by Lange, Brodsky, Goldenberg, B. and Z. Kwartin, Schwartz, Erstling, and Wohlberg, Hershman admits his guilt in losing his temper and in his choice of words. He will avoid acting in this manner in the future.

Motion by Goldenberg, seconded by Lange, to fine all who interrupt speakers at our meetings, is approved unanimously.

Motion by Schwartz, seconded by Brodsky, to express our approval of the conduct of our chairman (Glantz) of our last meeting is approved. Glantz takes over chair and reads copy of letter we sent Mr. Finestone. Letter meets with general approval. It is decided to continue discussion on improvisation at our next meeting, on May 16. The committee to arrange the program consists of Glantz, Goldenberg, Katchko, Roitman, and Friedman.

Cultural Meeting, May 16, 1939, at Ansche Chesed

The chairman, Glantz, stresses the importance of improvisation in our profession. Katchko discusses improvisation in the general context of Jewish music and its place in the cantorate. Wohlberg and Friedman then sing parts of "Zechor Beris Ovos" (Yom Kippur liturgy) as an example of spontaneous improvisation. Lange and Kwartin sing four Ya'alehs each. None of the above was informed previously which texts they would be asked to sing. *(Note: I believe Beimel made the selections.)* Beimel, Saltzman, Rappaport, Wohlberg, Lange, Katchko, Greenblatt, Roitman, and two laymen—Rabbi Meyer and Mr. A. Kessler—commented on the program. Glantz gives a thorough résumé of the opinions expressed during the evening.

Board of Directors, June 1, 1939, at Ansche Chesed

Glantz, chairman. Wohlberg and Katchko report on last meeting. (Note: the June and August 1939—last issue—of the *Chazanim Welt,* in Warsaw, contain articles by this writer on the programs and progress of the Cantors Cultural Organization.) Our next business meeting is set for June 7 at Steinway Hall, where reports on our finances and past activities will be given and nominations and election of officers will take place. The meeting will open at 8:15 and close at 11:30. Ringel and Friedman are appointed to find a suitable place for our final social meeting. It is decided that laymen be given the privilege to take the floor at our meetings.

Business Meeting, June 8, 1939, at Steinway Hall

Glantz, chairman. He reviews, with just pride and telling detail, the accomplishments of our organization during the past season. Schwartz thanks Glantz for excellent report. Wohlberg expresses appreciation of organization to Schwartz, Katchko, Glantz, Friedman, etc. Friedman reports that we have forty-seven paid-up members. Schwartz declares a balance of $11.04. Friedman, Lange, and Brodsky are optimistic regarding our future. Erstling urges taking our charter and bids us, in addition to our present work, to undertake regular organizational activities. In this view, he is supported by Saltzman, Schwartz, Lowy, Kwartin, Meisels, and Hershman. The last minimizes our achievements.

Katchko and Beimel stress need for cultural program. Putterman asks for active acceptance committee and for the establishment of a seminary. Glantz responds to all comments and denies our need for change of program. All previous decisions of our organization are reaffirmed by vote. It is decided that election of officers will be for period lasting until January 1940. Motion made by Brodsky to retain present officers. Schwartz amends that instead of a presidium, we elect a president and two vice presidents. Wohlberg advises retention of presidium, one of whom shall be permanent presiding officer. He so moves, motion carried. Due to late hour, election postponed for next meeting.

General Meeting and Election, June 14, 1939, at Ansche Chesed

Jassinowski, chairman. Minutes accepted. Election of officers: Schwartz, Hershman, Jassinowski, Beimel, and Putterman decline nomination for membership in the presidium. Glantz, Katchko, and Kwartin accept nomination for same. Upon motion by Putterman, they are elected by unanimous vote. Erstling moves that term for officers be for one year. Motion carried. Kwartin and Katchko decline nomination for office of presiding officer. Glantz accepts. Schwartz elected unanimously as treasurer. Upon motion made by Kwartin, seconded by Glantz, that Ringel is elected financial secretary; Wohlberg, recording secretary; Friedman, corresponding secretary. Glantz thanks Friedman for his devoted work. The following twelve are elected as members of the board of directors: Beimel, Ephros, Erstling, Goldenberg, Hershman, Jassinowski, Kritchmar, Lange, Putterman, Roitman, Steinberg, and Weisfeld. Putterman moves that acceptance committee review list of our membership.

Board of Directors, June 19, 1939, at Ansche Chesed

Glantz, chairman. Arrangements for proposed banquet on June 27 are discussed. Detailed report on hall (Broadway Caterers, 2528 Broadway) and meal (seven-course, roast spring chicken) is given by Ringel and is accepted unanimously. Wohlberg reports on program planned. Zeidel Rovner is to *bentsh*.

(Note: the following program appeared on the printed menu.)

> Opening Prayer: Jacob Schwartz
> National Hymns: David Putterman and Jacob Rappaport
> Introductory Remarks: Zavel Kwartin
> Toastmaster: Leib Glantz
> Symposium, "Cantorate Whither," G. Ephros, P. Jassinowski, A. Katchko, D. Roitman

MUSICAL PROGRAM: D. Brodsky, S. Meisels, D. Steinberg

Arrangement Committee: M. Erstling (chairman), I. Ringel, M. Wohlberg

(Note: on the back of my printed menu, I have some not quite distinct jottings. After Saul and Ida Meisels, I have in parentheses: Moussorgsky, "Shir Haro'eh," "Bin Ich Mir a Shneiderl." Following D. M. Steinberg, I have: "Hinei Ma Tov," "Ledor Vodor," "Ho'oseh Lonu" [Greenblatt, piano]. Ephros-Jassinowski? Brodsky's name is followed by: Werther, Massenet, and "Hatei Elo'ah." I distinctly recall Shmuel Postulow who had but recently arrived from Vienna. He was invited to sing and graciously consented to sing Sulzer's "V'se-erav" in G minor.)

Business Meeting, October 25, 1939, Steinway Hall

Glantz, chairman. After brief review of tragic situation in which Jewry finds itself, the chairman greets those present. He also reports of the discussion by the officers at a recent meeting, at his home, concerning the status of our organization. Roitman is in favor of our meetings to begin immediately after the holidays and believes that the time has arrived for a break with the *Farband*. Erstling is convinced that our solution lies in an independent, active, professional organization. Schwartz urges the continuance of our work in the area of culture, to establish a seminary and strengthen our position materially. Goldenberg stresses need for a seminary. Wohlberg sees no need in resigning from the *Farband* while our programs do not conflict.

According to Levitt, a seminary is not our most urgent need. A strong, independent organization is. Brodsky believes that the time is not yet ripe for a change in our status, unless we begin to agitate for all qualified cantors to join our ranks. He also advises that we endeavor to remedy the evils in the *Farband* "from within." Jassinowski wants our committees to prepare a program of activities similar to that of the past year. Katchko advocates cultural programs and feels that ultimately conditions will compel us to leave the *Farband*. Putterman considers our incessant preoccupation with the *Farband* to be absurd and would have us stick to our outlined program. Erstling reiterates his previous statement and proposes material help for our colleagues in need. Kwartin professes need for a charter, a seminary, and for consideration of economic problems. He thinks it advisable to express our views of the *Farband* at *Farband* meetings.

Glantz points out that our lack of comprehensive solution for cantorial problems prevents us, at this time, from going into competition with the *Farband* and declares all discussion of that organization to be pointless. Erstling moves (seconded by Schwartz) that we acquire a charter. Jassinowski moves that we refer question to board of directors. Latter motion accepted. Erstling moves acceptance of his previous suggestions. Motion accepted.

Kwartin wishes drive for membership. Schwartz asks those in arrears to pay their dues. It is unanimously decided not to undertake the giving of positions. The questions of charter, seminary, and monthly organ are referred to board of directors. A telegram from Hershman expresses regret that due to health, he is unable to attend this meeting.

Board of Directors, November 1, 1939

Glantz, chairman. It is decided that presidium will set date for next meeting and prepare program for it. The board unanimously decides to apply for a charter. Schwartz will call committee consisting of Putterman and Erstling to discuss necessary details for securing charter. A committee consisting of Putterman (chairman), Goldenberg, Jassinowski, Schwartz, Beimel, Roitman, Wohlberg, and presidium is to meet and bring in report on cantors' seminary.

After lengthy debate, the motion for a journal is tabled. A committee consisting of Jassinowski, Katchko, Glantz, Schwartz, and Beimel is authorized to bring in report regarding a proposed "cantors' radio hour."

Schwartz urges prompt payment of dues. Brodsky and Erstling are appointed to serve on membership committee, chaired by Putterman. Katchko moves for thanks to Mr. Zayde for the pictures of P. Minkowski and D. Nowakowski, which he presented to our organization. Brodsky is asked to visit Hershman, who is ill. The presidium is to act as permanent welfare committee and is to decide for which cases moral or financial help is to be extended. Wohlberg thinks it advisable to schedule all committee meetings on Mondays. Jassinowski, with cooperation of Ephros and Wohlberg, is entrusted to collect old and rare Jewish musical compositions and material of liturgical character.

(Note: the following minutes [without signature] were, I believe, written by David Putterman, who, as I recall, forwarded them to me.)

Minutes of Membership Committee of the Cantor Ministers Cultural Organization held on Monday, November 6, 1939, at 1 p.m. in the study of Rev. Katchko. Those present were Cantors Erstling, Putterman, Ringel, and Schwartz. The meeting was presided over by Cantor Putterman. The committee decided to make the following recommendations to the board of directors for its consideration and adoption.

1. That membership dues shall commence annually as of October 1, and that those who made payments of $4 or more since June 1939, will be credited as of October 1. That hereafter, dues shall be paid in sums not less than semiannually and that those who are accepted for membership during the year shall be charged on a pro-rata basis.
2. All those who are at present members of the organization shall be required to sign application blanks.
3. All new applicants for membership will be required to sign application blanks accompanied by check in payment of six months' dues. These applications must be signed by two members in good standing. All applications will then be referred to the membership committee for approval and will then be submitted to the board of directors, whose decision shall be final.

4. No applicant will be considered, unless he has been actively engaged as cantor, for a period of at least three years, in the employ of a regularly incorporated synagogue.

5. Members who are in arrears for six months will be given two weeks' notice, and if their dues are not paid within that period they will be automatically suspended.

Cultural Meeting, November 16, 1939, at Steinway Hall

Glantz, chairman. The chairman introduces (in Hebrew), the guest speaker, Dr. Mordecai Sandberg of Palestine, who is a well-known composer and eminent musicologist. Dr. Sandberg gives a talk (in English) entitled "Tonality and the Cantorial Art." He emphasizes the importance of the quarter-tone system in recording ancient music and explains his own invention: the universal microtonal system. General discussion (mostly in Yiddish) and question-and-answer period follows. Chairman expresses appreciation of our organization to Dr. Sandberg for his illuminating lecture.

Board of Directors Meeting, November 30, 1939

Glantz, chairman. It is decided to invite Dr. Sandberg again for a lecture and to pay transportation expenses for his specially constructed instrument needed to illustrate his microtonal system. A motion is accepted to secure subscriptions among cantors, amounting to $100, for publishing two of Dr. Sandberg's songs. Our presidium is to review the songs. The sum of $32 raised among those present. Putterman reports on meeting of Membership Committee held on November 6. (Note: see minutes of that meeting above.) It is reported that a charter for our organization will cost $46 (approximately). Attorney, Miss E. Schwartz, daughter of our colleague, offered her services gratis, in obtaining it. Putterman and Glantz will help in preparing its content and character.

Putterman reports that seminary committee, in view of present general situation, recommends the establishment of weekly courses in 1) *nusha'ot* and 2) history of liturgy. Steinberg would add 3) elementary theory of music. It is also suggested that a complete service and *siddur* be composed by and for our members. Proposals are referred back to committees for further consideration.

Cultural Meeting, December 12, in Social Room of Ansche Chesed

Glantz, chairman. (A large audience is assembled.) The chairman stresses rejuvenating character of the Hanukkah festival and bids our colleagues to assist in the rebirth of cantorial art through medium of Cantors Ministers Cultural Organization and its programs. Mr. J. Joels, well-known pianist, then performs M. Milner's "Beim Reben Tzu Melaveh Malkeh," a fantasy on Jewish folk melodies.

At the behest of the chairman, the audience rises in silent memory of our many martyrs who died in distant lands. D. M. Steinberg lights the Hanukkah candles and chants the appropriate passages. The guest speaker of the evening, Dr. Sandberg, delivers an address on his microtonal system. The latter subdivides our present diatonic and chromatic tone system into fourth-, twelfth- and sixteenth-tone intervals. This system would, according to the speaker, eliminate the many faulty divisions of the present scale and would greatly facilitate a true-to-pitch accompaniment of the singer. By his specially built (organ-like) instrument, the speaker illustrates his theory.

A. Katchko then sings Sandberg's setting of "Chazon Yeshayaku," accompanied by J. Joels. D. Roitman sings two of his own compositions: "Yehi Rotzon" and "Yisgadal," which are analyzed by the speaker in light of the microtonal system. The chairman thanks the speaker. Refreshments are served in the anteroom.

Board of Directors, December 18, 1939, at Ansche Chesed

Glantz, chairman. Schwartz and Glantz report on their meeting with attorney Eleanor Schwartz and read the draft of the charter prepared by her. Glantz, Schwartz, and Putterman are requested to meet with her regarding the final draft, which will then be submitted to the general body.

An organization seal is recommended in the form of a circle within which our name (Cantors Ministers Cultural Organization) in English will appear on top; Chazanim Kultur Organizatsia at the bottom; and Histadrut Chazanim Tarbutit in the center. Beimel proposes a Sulzer memorial program commemorating the fiftieth yahrzeit of the great cantor and composer. Proposal unanimously accepted. Presidium requested to prepare program for next cultural meeting.

Board of Directors, December 27, 1939, at Ansche Chesed

Glantz, chairman. It is decided that those of our officers (Jassinowski, Katchko, Kritchmar, B. Kwartin, Roitman, Steinberg. and Wohlberg) whose names appear on the stationery of the *Farband* as members of its advisory board, in violation of our by-laws, immediately request the withdrawal of their names from that board. Copies of these requests are to be given to our secretary. Glantz reports on his visit with Hershman, who is ill. It is decided to postpone our next business meeting to January 10, 1940, when further collections for printing two Sandberg songs will be taken up. A committee, with full power, consisting of presidium, Beimel, Jassinowski, Putterman, and Wohlberg, is appointed to prepare program for Sulzer memorial. Putterman suggests three subjects for courses to be given within our organization:

1. *Hazzanut,* which will include: cantillation, history and art of *hazzanut,* history of Jewish music, and history of liturgy.
2. Music, which will include theory, harmony, and art of voice.
3. Hebrew, which will include conversation and *dinei tefillah.*

He also proposes the inauguration of courses consisting of Hebrew, history of liturgy, *nusha'ot,* and theory of music on January 15, and every week thereafter. Each course to consist of 12 lectures to be paid for (at $2) by the students. Teachers are to receive not more than $25 per course. Beimel, Ephros, and Katchko are proposed as instructors. Kwartin urges the start of a drive for a large relief fund to be combined with the forming of an Agudat Chovevei Chazanim, in which connection he offers considerable (financial and other) help. Kwartin appointed chairman of this fund-raising committee. School committee will consist of Putterman, presidium, and Wohlberg.

Business Meeting, January 10, 1940, at Steinway Hall

Glantz, chairman. Minutes of previous meeting accepted with corrections. Miss E. Schwartz, attorney, reads draft of charter, which is discussed and accepted. However, minor changes are to be made by board of directors. Those signing certificate for charter will consist of organizers and officers. Further collection for Sandberg's songs is taken up. Recess declared for payment of dues.

Glantz requests all to visit Hershman before his departure for Florida. Kazimirsky, president of Union of Synagogue Conductors, asks—through Glantz—our members to engage only union choir leaders. Motion made by Schwartz, seconded by Kaplow, to postpone Sulzer meeting to later date. Schwartz promises to endeavor to secure his temple (B'nai Jeshurun) and choir gratis for this affair. Putterman, Brodsky, Beimel, and Glantz will discuss this proposal with Schwartz.

Board of Directors Meeting, January 24, 1940, at Ansche Chesed

Glantz, chairman. It is decided to hold Sulzer meeting at Shaare Zedek (Roitman's) Congregation, 93rd Street and Broadway, on February 7, 1940. Acknowledgment, received from Schwartz, of telegram we sent upon completion of twenty-five years of service with B'nai Jeshurun. Mr. Zalis, the choir leader, here at the invitation of our board of directors, is asked whether he can prepare his choir for Sulzer meeting and what the cost would be. He estimates $50. Chairman thanks him for his readiness to assist us. Schwartz proposes to supply his choir and organist for sum of $25. His proposal accepted with profuse thanks. Letter received from *Farband* asking for committee of our organization to meet with their committee. Our committee will consist of presidium and Schwartz. It is understood that no proposal or commitments are to be made by our committee. Meeting will take place in Schwartz's office on Monday.

Board of Directors Meeting, January 31, 1940, at Home of Glantz

Glantz reports on our meeting with *Farband*, where the latter proposed amalgamation on following conditions: (1) that they resign from the American Federation of Labor; 2) only yearly positions will be given by their placement committee; and 3) that those of their members who are unworthy of our profession are expelled. Weisser proposed the formation of a board of presidium consisting of representatives of the three existing organizations. Putterman moves, seconded by Ringel, to refer these proposals to our next board of directors meeting. Motion carried.

Erstling relates that yesterday's meeting of Sulzer memorial committee, with officers, broke up in disagreement. Glantz, in a detailed report, regrets the lack of cooperation of Katchko and Wohlberg. The latter (two) reply to the accusation. Schwartz, Beimel, Brodsky, Erstling, and Ringel express their views. (See note below.) It is decided to distribute circulars in various synagogues (re: Sulzer meeting) and to invite music organizations and choruses. Ringel and Wohlberg are to attend to printing and distribution of letters and circulars. Goldenberg will call choir leaders. Beimel and Jassinowski will secure press notices and, with Glantz, will write articles. Schwartz had ordered a piano. Erstling will act as chairman of reception committee.

(Note: While the nature of the precise incident causing the disagreement between Glantz and myself escapes me, I clearly recall my criticism of his occasional indulgence in authoritarian and dictatorial attitudes. Whether Katchko sided with me on this issue, or had another reason for a fallout with Glantz, I do not remember. M. W.)

MEMORIAL MEETING

In Honor of the Great
Cantor and Composer
SOLOMON SULZER
on the
Fiftieth Anniversary of His Death
arranged by the
Cantors Ministers Cultural Organization
Wednesday, February 7, 1940
8:30 p.m.—Shevat 28, 5700
at Temple Shaare Zedek
93rd Street at Broadway, New York

PROGRAM

Invocation	Rabbi Elias Solomon
Introductory Remarks	Pinchos Jassinowski
Sulzer: The Cantor	Chairman Leib Glantz
"Al Naharos Bovel," by S. Sulzer	Choir of Congregation B'nai Jeshurun, Jacob Schwartz conducting
Musical Contributions of Sulzer	Lazar Saminsky
"B'leil Zeh Yivkoyun," by S. Sulzer	B'nai Jeshurun Choir
Sulzer: The Man and His Work	Jacob Beimel

MEMORIAL SERVICE

"Schochnei Votei Chomer," "Shivisi," and "Emes Ki Ato Hu Yotzrom," by S. Sulzer	Cantors Ensemble, consisting of B Brodsky, A. Goldberg, H. Greenblatt, A. Hyman, S. Meisels, M. Postulow, W. Sauler, M. Wohlberg, M. Lexandrowitch, and M. Shanok; Adolph Katchko, conducting
"Eil Molei Rachamim"	David Roitman, cantor of Shaare Zedek
Benediction	Rabbi M. Goldberg

Arrangement Committee: M. Erstling, I. Ringel, and M. Wohlberg

―――――∽―――――

During the past two years, the status of the cantor was the subject of briefs and arguments before the courts and at the hearings of various governmental bodies. At issue were such vital matters as: (1) the right of the cantor to solemnize marriages; (2) his ministerial status regarding Social Security; and (3) his inclusion in the ranks of those entitled to a tax-exempt parsonage allowance. Judaism in aspects such as structure, dogma, clergy, laity, and so on, is not comparable with Christianity. Our Jewish authorities who, when approached during this dispute, stated that the terms "minister," "clergy," "ordination," and "license," do not fit Jewish concepts, and hence are inappropriate for the cantor, were absolutely correct. However, their statement would have been received with greater warmth and would have carried more conviction if they had indicated that these terms were equally inappropriate to the rabbinate. The numerous religious, ethical, moral, and scholarly requirements made of the cantor in talmudic and rabbinic literature serve as ample evidence that throughout our history this oldest Jewish functionary was indeed considered a religious functionary, as was his task a melekhet hakodesh, *a holy task. Thus, both in function as well as in image, we are here confronted with the equivalent of the clergyman or minister in Christian denominations.*

—Wohlberg, **Pirkei Hazzanut,** *The Cantors Voice* 17, no. 1 (September 1966)

―――――∽―――――

APPENDIX E
Musical Autographs

Avot–Gevurot Melodies

Max Wohlberg
arr. Charles Davidson

Appendix E 149

Appendix E 153

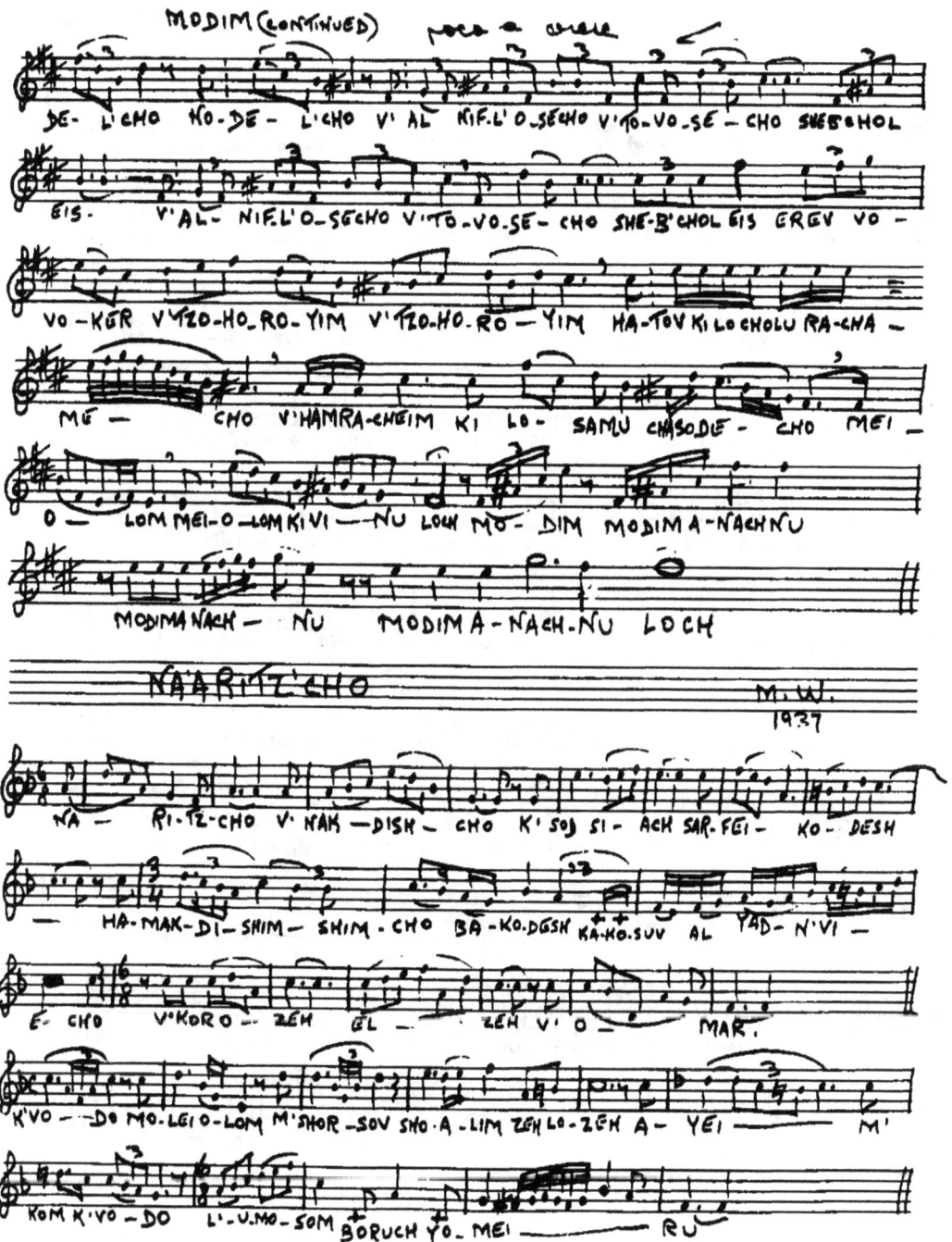

Appendix E

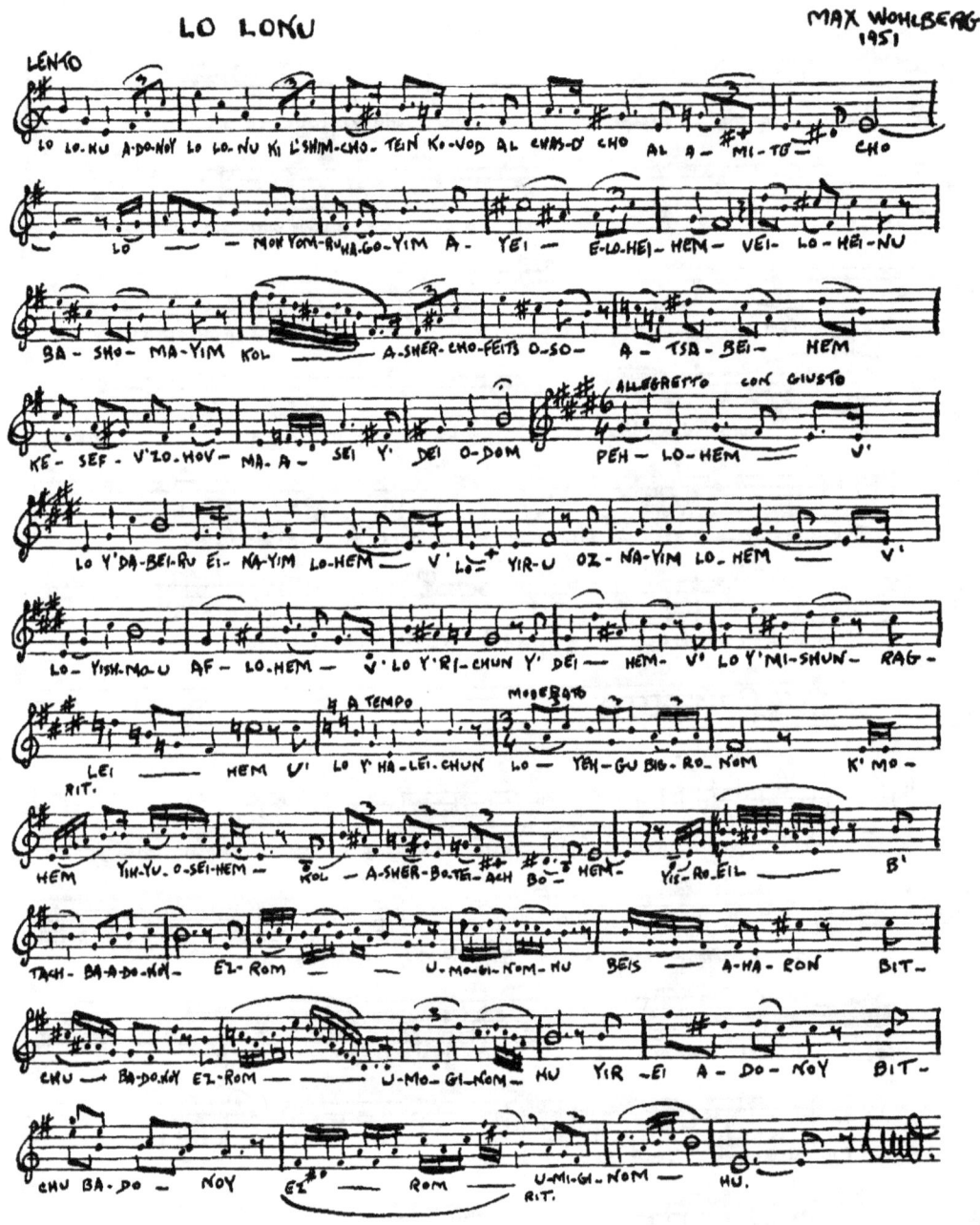

Appendix E 157

www.ingramcontent.com/pod-product-compliance
Lightning Source LLC
Chambersburg PA
CBHW080339170426
43194CB00014B/2623